DR. ERNESTO LEE

AI and the Art of Productive Struggle

How AI Reshapes Teaching and Learning

First published by Learning Science Publishing 2025

Copyright © 2025 by Dr. Ernesto Lee

All rights reserved. No part of this publication may be reproduced, stored or transmitted in any form or by any means, electronic, mechanical, photocopying, recording, scanning, or otherwise without written permission from the publisher. It is illegal to copy this book, post it to a website, or distribute it by any other means without permission.

Dr. Ernesto Lee asserts the moral right to be identified as the author of this work.

Dr. Ernesto Lee has no responsibility for the persistence or accuracy of URLs for external or third-party Internet Websites referred to in this publication and does not guarantee that any content on such Websites is, or will remain, accurate or appropriate.

Designations used by companies to distinguish their products are often claimed as trademarks. All brand names and product names used in this book and on its cover are trade names, service marks, trademarks and registered trademarks of their respective owners. The publishers and the book are not associated with any product or vendor mentioned in this book. None of the companies referenced within the book have endorsed the book.

First edition

ISBN: 978-1-942864-48-6

This book was professionally typeset on Reedsy. Find out more at reedsy.com

To my high school guidance counselor who tried to convince me that I wasn't college material and that if I was a "good boy" then maybe she would help me get a job at the Pueblo Train Depot shoveling coal.

No thanks.

But thank you for lighting the fire.

Contents

Preface ii
Acknowledgments viii
1 The Productive Friction Revolution - Why AI's Greatest Gift... 1
2 Meta-Prompting - Summoning the Wisdom of the Sages ... 17
3 System Prompts - Engineering AI Personalities with Academic... 40
4 Custom Learning Environments - Your Knowledge, Your... 63
5 Multi-Modal Learning - When AI Speaks Your Language ... 90
6 Screen Sharing Intelligence - When AI Sees What You See ... 114
7 Visual Intelligence - When AI Creates What You Can't Imagine 141
8 Agentic Content Creation - When AI Becomes Your Teaching... 161
9 Conversational App Development - English as the Hottest... 182
10 LearningScience.ai - The Purpose-Built Educational AI... 201
About the Author 220

Preface

"The job of a teacher is to guide the social process of learning. AI is simply another tool that assists the teacher in this process." — Dr. Ernesto Lee

Why Teachers Will Never Be Replaced by AI

In the summer of 2023, I sat in a faculty meeting where a colleague nervously asked the question that haunts educators everywhere: "Will AI replace teachers?" The room fell silent. You could feel the collective anxiety of dedicated professionals who had devoted their lives to education, suddenly wondering if their expertise had become obsolete overnight.

My answer surprised them: "Teachers will never be replaced by AI—because we've fundamentally misunderstood what teachers actually do."

The fear of AI replacement stems from a profound misconception about the nature of teaching. Too many people believe that teaching is about delivering information, when in reality, teaching is about guiding the social process of learning. This distinction changes everything.

The Tool Analogy That Changes Everything

Let me share an analogy that has shaped my entire approach to educational AI. Think about a shovel and a bulldozer. Both are tools designed to move dirt. One is more technologically advanced than the other, but they both operate on the same core principle: move dirt.

The bulldozer replaces the shovel—it's faster, more efficient, and can handle bigger jobs. But here's the crucial insight: the bulldozer doesn't replace the human. It amplifies human capability. The construction worker doesn't become obsolete; they become more powerful.

Now consider this: a book and AI are like the shovel and the bulldozer. The core operating principle is the same: educate. AI is simply a more technologically advanced version of a book. It can access more information, respond to questions, adapt to individual needs, and provide interactive experiences that static text cannot.

AI can replace the book, but it cannot replace the educator.

The Irreplaceable Human Element

Why? Because the fundamental job of an educator has never been to be a walking encyclopedia or a human textbook. The job of a teacher is to guide the social process of learning.

Learning is inherently social. It happens in relationships, through dialogue, within communities of practice. It requires empathy, cultural understanding, emotional intelligence, and the ability to recognize when a student needs encouragement, challenge, or a completely different approach.

AI can provide information. Teachers provide transformation.

AI can answer questions. Teachers ask the right questions. AI can explain concepts. Teachers inspire curiosity. AI can provide feedback. Teachers provide hope.

The Partnership Revolution

This book is not about AI versus teachers. It's about AI with teachers. It's about recognizing that the most powerful educational experiences happen when human wisdom guides artificial intelligence.

Throughout these pages, you'll discover how to:

- Use AI to amplify your pedagogical expertise, not replace it
- Create learning experiences that combine technological power with human insight

- Maintain the irreplaceable human elements of teaching while leveraging AI's capabilities
- Guide students in developing both digital literacy and critical thinking skills

The Social Process of Learning

Learning is not a transaction—it's a transformation. And transformation requires the kind of nuanced, culturally responsive, emotionally intelligent guidance that only human educators can provide.

When a student struggles with calculus, they don't just need the correct mathematical procedure. They need someone who can recognize their frustration, understand their learning style, connect the concept to their interests, and provide the encouragement necessary to persist through difficulty.

When a student asks a question, they're not just seeking information. They're seeking connection, validation, and guidance from someone who cares about their growth as a human being.

This is the work that AI cannot do. This is the work that makes teachers irreplaceable.

The Enhanced Educator

But here's what AI can do: it can free teachers from the routine tasks that consume so much of our time and energy. It can provide personalized practice for students, generate creative lesson materials, offer instant feedback on assignments, and create interactive learning experiences that would be impossible to develop manually.

When AI handles the information delivery, teachers can focus on what we do best: inspiring, guiding, mentoring, and transforming lives.

This is not about making teachers obsolete. This is about making teachers more powerful than ever before.

The Future We're Building

The future of education is not human versus machine. It's human with machine. It's educators who understand how to guide AI to serve learning rather than replace it.

In this future, teachers become:

- Learning Experience Designers who craft meaningful educational journeys
- AI Orchestrators who know how to leverage technology for pedagogical purposes
- Relationship Builders who create the human connections that make learning meaningful
- Critical Thinking Guides who help students navigate an AI-enhanced world
- Wisdom Cultivators who transform information into understanding

The Invitation

This book is an invitation to step confidently into that future. You are not being replaced—you are being enhanced. Your expertise is not becoming obsolete—it's becoming more valuable than ever.

The students of tomorrow will need teachers who can help them think critically about AI-generated content, who can guide them in asking better questions, who can help them develop the uniquely human skills that no algorithm can replicate.

They will need teachers who understand that the goal is not to compete with AI, but to dance with it.

A Personal Note

As I've developed LearningScience.ai and worked with educators across South Florida and beyond, I've seen the transformation that happens when teachers embrace AI as a powerful tool rather than fear it as a threat.

I've watched a chemistry teacher use AI to create personalized lab simulations for each student. I've seen a history professor use AI to generate primary source documents for role-playing exercises. I've observed language arts teachers use AI to provide instant feedback on student writing, freeing them to focus on developing voice and creativity.

In every case, the teacher became more effective, not less relevant.

The Promise of This Book

The chapters that follow will show you exactly how to harness the power of AI while maintaining the irreplaceable human elements that make great teaching possible. You'll learn practical strategies, see real examples, and discover how to create learning experiences that are both technologically sophisticated and deeply human.

This is not about replacing teachers with AI. This is about empowering teachers through AI.

The bulldozer didn't replace the construction worker—it made them capable of building skyscrapers instead of just moving dirt. AI won't replace teachers—it will make us capable of transforming education in ways we never thought possible.

The future belongs to educators who understand this distinction.

Welcome to that future. Welcome to teaching and learning with AI.

Dr. Ernesto Lee

College Professor, South Florida

Founder, LearningScience.ai

2025

Acknowledgments

To my family, both blood and chosen.

You have been my foundation, my inspiration, and my strength throughout this journey. Your unwavering support, endless encouragement, and belief in the power of education have made this work possible.

To my blood family, who taught me that *love transcends circumstances and that education is the one thing no one can ever take away from you*. Your sacrifices, wisdom, and resilience shaped the educator I became.

To my chosen family, who *welcomed me with open hearts and minds, who challenged my thinking, celebrated my victories, and stood by me through every struggle*. You showed me that family is not just about where you come from, but about who chooses to walk alongside you.

Together, you have created a community of learning, growth, and possibility that extends far beyond any classroom or institution. You have taught me that the most profound education happens in relationships, and that the greatest lessons are learned through love.

This book exists because of your *collective faith in the transformative power of education* and your belief that every student deserves a teacher who sees their potential, regardless of what others might say.

Thank you for being my teachers, my students, and my inspiration.

With love and gratitude,

Ernesto

1

The Productive Friction Revolution - Why AI's Greatest Gift to Education Isn't What You Think

"The cave you fear to enter holds the treasure you seek." — *Joseph Campbell*

The Calculus Crisis That Changed Everything

Professor Sarah Chen had always prided herself on being an innovative educator. When ChatGPT burst onto the scene in late 2022, she was among the first faculty members at her university to embrace AI in her calculus courses. Her students were struggling with complex integration problems, and she thought she had found the perfect solution: an AI tutor that could provide instant, step-by-step solutions to any mathematical challenge.

The results were immediate and seemingly miraculous. Student satisfaction scores soared. Office hours became nearly empty as students could get instant help at 3 AM. Homework completion rates reached 100% for the first time in her teaching career. Professor Chen felt like she had revolutionized mathematics education.

But then came the midterm exam.

Despite months of AI-assisted homework with perfect completion rates, her students performed worse than any class she had taught in fifteen years. The very students who had been confidently solving complex integrals with AI assistance couldn't handle basic derivative problems without technological support. **The AI hadn't made them better at calculus—it had made them dependent on getting answers without understanding.**

Professor Chen had discovered what would become the central paradox of AI in education: **the very feature that makes AI most appealing—its ability to eliminate friction—is precisely what makes it most dangerous to learning.**

The Friction Paradox: When Ease Becomes the Enemy

In our rush to embrace artificial intelligence in education, we have stumbled upon a fundamental contradiction that strikes at the heart of how learning actually works. **AI's superpower is removing friction, but friction is where learning lives.**

This isn't a minor technical glitch that can be fixed with better prompts or smarter algorithms. This is a profound philosophical challenge that forces us to reconsider everything we think we know about the relationship between technology and learning. **We are facing the first technology in human history that is so good at thinking that it can prevent us from learning how to think.**

The friction paradox manifests in countless ways across educational contexts. When students ask AI to solve their math problems, they get perfect solutions but miss the cognitive struggle that builds mathematical reasoning. When they request essay outlines, they receive well-structured arguments but bypass the messy process of developing their own ideas. When they seek explanations of complex concepts, they get clear, polished responses but avoid the productive confusion that leads to deep understanding.

The irony is devastating: the smoother we make the learning process, the less learning actually occurs.

This paradox isn't limited to obvious cases of academic dishonesty or shortcut-seeking. Even well-intentioned educational uses of AI can inadvertently eliminate the very cognitive processes that make learning meaningful and lasting. **We have created tools so powerful at providing answers that they can rob students of the opportunity to develop the capacity to find answers themselves.**

The Neuroscience of Necessary Struggle

To understand why friction is essential for learning, we must examine what actually happens in the brain when genuine learning occurs. Neuroscientific research has consistently demonstrated that **learning is not the acquisition of information—it is the physical rewiring of neural pathways through effortful cognitive processing.**

When students encounter challenging problems that require sustained mental effort, their brains undergo measurable structural changes. The struggle to understand difficult concepts literally builds new neural connections, strengthens existing pathways, and develops the cognitive architecture necessary for independent thinking. **The brain grows stronger not from getting answers, but from the work of seeking answers.**

This process, known as "desirable difficulty" in cognitive science research, requires what educational psychologists call "productive struggle"—the optimal level of cognitive challenge that promotes learning without causing overwhelming frustration. **Productive struggle is the sweet spot where confusion transforms into understanding, where effort becomes expertise, and where temporary discomfort leads to lasting competence.**

But AI, in its current implementation in most educational contexts, eliminates this productive struggle entirely. **When students can get instant answers to complex questions, their brains never engage in the effortful processing that creates learning.** The neural pathways that should be strengthened through cognitive challenge remain underdeveloped, leaving students with the illusion of understanding but without the underlying cognitive capacity.

The implications are profound and troubling. **We are creating a generation of students who can access any answer but cannot generate original thoughts, who can find any solution but cannot solve novel problems, who can retrieve any information but cannot create new knowledge.**

The Dependency Trap: How AI Creates Learned Helplessness

The most insidious aspect of the friction paradox is how quickly students become dependent on AI assistance. What begins as occasional help with difficult problems rapidly evolves into an inability to engage in independent cognitive work. **AI doesn't just solve problems for students—it teaches them that problems should be solved by something other than their own thinking.**

This phenomenon, which we might call "cognitive outsourcing," represents a new form of learned helplessness specifically adapted to the AI age. Students begin to believe that their own thinking is inadequate, that their natural cognitive processes are too slow and inefficient compared to AI capabilities. **They lose confidence not just in their ability to find answers, but in their right to struggle with questions.**

The dependency trap is particularly dangerous because it feels like empowerment. Students experience the immediate gratification of getting correct answers, the relief of avoiding cognitive discomfort, and the efficiency of completing assignments quickly. **The very features that make AI feel helpful in the short term are precisely what makes it harmful in the long term.**

This creates what educational researchers call a "competence illusion"—students feel knowledgeable and capable while using AI assistance, but this feeling evaporates the moment they must perform independently. **They mistake access to intelligence for the development of intelligence, confusing the ability to prompt AI with the ability to think critically.**

The dependency trap is self-reinforcing. As students become more reliant on AI assistance, their tolerance for cognitive struggle decreases. Problems that would have been manageable challenges become overwhelming obstacles. **The more AI helps, the more help students need, creating a downward spiral of cognitive dependence.**

The Authenticity Crisis: When Learning Becomes Performance

The widespread adoption of AI in education has created what we might call an "authenticity crisis"—a fundamental uncertainty about what constitutes genuine learning versus sophisticated mimicry. **When students can produce work that appears to demonstrate understanding but actually represents AI capability, the entire foundation of educational assessment crumbles.**

This crisis extends far beyond concerns about academic dishonesty. Even when students use AI tools openly and with good intentions, the line between their thinking and AI thinking becomes increasingly blurred. **We are losing the ability to distinguish between what students know and what they can access, between what they can do and what they can prompt AI to do.**

The authenticity crisis is particularly acute in writing-intensive disciplines. When students can generate essays, research papers, and creative works with AI assistance, how do we evaluate their actual writing ability, critical thinking skills, or creative capacity? **The very artifacts we have traditionally used to assess learning may no longer provide reliable evidence of student capability.**

But the crisis runs deeper than assessment challenges. **When students cannot distinguish between their own thinking and AI-generated content, they lose touch with their own intellectual identity.** They begin to doubt the value of their own ideas, the validity of their own reasoning processes, and the worth of their own creative expressions.

This creates a profound psychological challenge that extends far beyond academic contexts. **Students are developing an external locus of intellectual control, believing that real thinking happens outside**

themselves rather than within their own minds. They are becoming strangers to their own cognitive processes, uncertain about their own intellectual capabilities and potential.

The Illusion of Efficiency: Why Faster Isn't Better

One of the most seductive aspects of AI in education is its promise of efficiency. Students can complete assignments faster, get help immediately, and access information instantly. Educators can generate lesson plans quickly, provide feedback efficiently, and create assessments rapidly. **But efficiency in education is often the enemy of effectiveness.**

Learning is inherently inefficient. It requires time for reflection, space for confusion, and patience with the messy process of understanding development. **The cognitive processes that create lasting learning—struggle, reflection, synthesis, and application—cannot be rushed without being undermined.**

When we optimize for efficiency in education, we inadvertently optimize against learning. **The time students save by using AI to complete assignments quickly is precisely the time their brains need to process, integrate, and internalize new knowledge.** The immediate feedback AI provides eliminates the productive delay that allows students to develop self-assessment skills and metacognitive awareness.

The efficiency illusion is particularly dangerous because it aligns with broader cultural values that prioritize speed, productivity, and immediate results. **We have imported the metrics of business and technology into education, measuring success by throughput rather than depth, by completion rather than comprehension, by speed rather than understanding.**

But education is not a manufacturing process where faster production leads to better outcomes. **Learning is a biological process that requires time, repetition, and gradual development.** When we try to accelerate learning beyond its natural pace, we don't create more learning—we create the illusion of learning while undermining the cognitive processes that make real learning possible.

The Personalization Paradox: How AI Customization Can Limit Growth

Another compelling promise of AI in education is its ability to provide personalized learning experiences tailored to individual student needs, preferences, and learning styles. This sounds ideal in theory, but in practice, it can create what we might call the "personalization paradox"—**the more AI adapts to student preferences, the less students develop the ability to adapt to new challenges.**

When AI systems continuously adjust content difficulty, presentation style, and pacing to match student comfort zones, they inadvertently create intellectual echo chambers. **Students become accustomed to receiving information in their preferred format and at their optimal challenge level, but real-world learning rarely accommodates such preferences.**

The personalization paradox is particularly problematic because it can prevent students from developing intellectual resilience and adaptability. **When AI removes all sources of cognitive discomfort, students never learn to cope with confusion, frustration, or uncertainty—emotions that are essential for navigating complex real-world challenges.**

Moreover, excessive personalization can limit exposure to diverse perspectives, alternative approaches, and challenging viewpoints. **When AI systems optimize for student engagement and satisfaction, they may inadvertently narrow rather than broaden intellectual horizons.** Students receive content that confirms their existing beliefs and approaches rather than content that challenges them to grow.

The most insidious aspect of the personalization paradox is that it feels like good teaching. **Responsive, adaptive, individualized instruction appears to embody the best principles of effective education.** But when taken to extremes, personalization can become a form of intellectual coddling that prevents students from developing the cognitive flexibility and resilience they need for lifelong learning.

The Metacognitive Meltdown: When Students Stop Thinking About Thinking

Perhaps the most profound consequence of AI's friction-removal in education is what we might call a "metacognitive meltdown"—the erosion of students' ability to monitor, evaluate, and regulate their own thinking processes. **When AI handles the cognitive heavy lifting, students lose touch with their own mental processes and become unable to direct their own learning.**

Metacognition—thinking about thinking—is arguably the most important skill students can develop. It enables them to assess their own understanding, identify knowledge gaps, select appropriate learning strategies, and monitor their progress toward learning goals. **Metacognitive awareness is what transforms students from passive recipients of information into active directors of their own intellectual development.**

But AI assistance can short-circuit metacognitive development in subtle and dangerous ways. When students can get immediate answers to questions, they never develop the ability to assess whether they truly understand a concept. When AI provides step-by-step solutions, students never learn to monitor their own problem-solving processes. **When external intelligence handles cognitive tasks, internal intelligence atrophies.**

The metacognitive meltdown is particularly concerning because it affects students' ability to learn independently throughout their lives. **Students who become dependent on AI assistance may never develop the self-awareness and self-regulation skills necessary for autonomous learning.** They may graduate with degrees but without the capacity for intellectual growth and adaptation that lifelong learning requires.

This creates a fundamental paradox: **the technology that promises to make students smarter may actually be making them less capable of becoming smarter on their own.** AI can provide access to vast amounts of information and sophisticated analysis, but it cannot develop the internal cognitive processes that enable students to think critically, creatively, and independently.

The Creativity Catastrophe: How AI Assistance Stifles Innovation

One of the most troubling consequences of AI's friction-removal in education is its impact on student creativity and innovation. **When AI can generate ideas, solutions, and creative works on demand, students lose the opportunity to develop their own creative capacities.** The struggle to generate original ideas, the frustration of creative blocks, and the satisfaction of breakthrough moments are all essential components of creative development that AI assistance can inadvertently eliminate.

Creativity is not just about producing novel outputs—it's about developing the cognitive processes that enable innovation. **Creative thinking requires tolerance for ambiguity, comfort with uncertainty, and persistence through frustration.** These capacities can only be developed through direct experience with creative challenges, not through observation of AI-generated solutions.

When students can prompt AI to generate creative works, they miss the iterative process of idea development that builds creative capacity. **They see the final product but not the cognitive journey that creates it.** They experience the satisfaction of having a creative work but not the growth that comes from creating it themselves.

The creativity catastrophe is particularly concerning in fields that depend on human innovation and original thinking. **If students never develop their own creative capacities, who will generate the novel ideas, innovative solutions, and artistic expressions that drive human progress?** We risk creating a generation that can appreciate and modify AI-generated creativity but cannot originate creative works themselves.

Moreover, creativity is deeply connected to personal identity and self-expression. **When students outsource their creative work to AI, they lose opportunities for self-discovery and personal growth that come through creative expression.** They may never discover their own unique perspectives, voices, and creative potential.

The Social Learning Collapse: How AI Isolates Learners

Learning is fundamentally a social process. Students develop understanding through discussion, debate, collaboration, and peer interaction. **The friction of working through disagreements, explaining ideas to others, and building on collective knowledge is essential for deep learning.** But AI assistance can inadvertently isolate students from these crucial social learning experiences.

When students can get immediate answers from AI, they have less motivation to seek help from peers, participate in study groups, or engage in collaborative problem-solving. **AI becomes a substitute for human interaction rather than a supplement to it.** Students may prefer the non-judgmental, always-available assistance of AI over the more complex and sometimes challenging interactions with classmates and instructors.

This social learning collapse has profound implications for students' development of communication skills, empathy, and collaborative capacity. **Learning to explain ideas clearly, listen to different perspectives, and work through disagreements are essential life skills that can only be developed through human interaction.** When AI assistance reduces these interactions, students miss crucial opportunities for social and emotional development.

Moreover, social learning provides essential feedback mechanisms that help students calibrate their understanding. **When students explain concepts to peers, they discover gaps in their knowledge. When they encounter different perspectives, they refine their thinking.** AI assistance, no matter how sophisticated, cannot fully replicate the dynamic, unpredictable, and emotionally rich experience of learning with and from other humans.

The social learning collapse is particularly concerning in an era when collaboration and communication skills are increasingly valued in professional contexts. **Students who become accustomed to AI assistance may struggle to work effectively in teams, communicate complex ideas clearly, or navigate the social dynamics of collaborative work.**

The Assessment Apocalypse: When We Can No Longer Measure Learning

The widespread availability of AI assistance has created what we might call an "assessment apocalypse"—a fundamental breakdown in our ability to measure student learning accurately. **Traditional assessment methods, from homework assignments to research papers to problem sets, may no longer provide reliable evidence of student capability when AI assistance is readily available.**

This crisis extends far beyond concerns about academic dishonesty. Even when students use AI tools openly and appropriately, it becomes increasingly difficult to determine what represents their own thinking versus AI capability. **We are losing the ability to distinguish between what students can do independently and what they can accomplish with technological assistance.**

The assessment apocalypse forces us to confront fundamental questions about what we are trying to measure and why. **If the goal of education is to develop human capability, then assessments must measure human performance, not human-AI collaboration.** But if the goal is to prepare students for a world where AI assistance is ubiquitous, then perhaps our assessment methods need to evolve accordingly.

This uncertainty creates practical challenges for educators who must assign grades, provide feedback, and make decisions about student progress. **How do we evaluate student work when we cannot be certain of its authorship? How do we provide meaningful feedback when we don't know which aspects of the work represent student thinking?**

The assessment apocalypse also has implications for credentialing and certification. **If degrees and certificates are meant to certify student capability, what do they mean when student work may have been significantly influenced by AI assistance?** Employers, graduate schools, and other stakeholders may begin to question the validity of traditional educational credentials.

The Wisdom Gap: Knowledge Without Understanding

Perhaps the most profound consequence of AI's friction-removal in education is the creation of what we might call a "wisdom gap"—the growing distance between access to information and the development of wisdom. **AI can provide students with vast amounts of knowledge and sophisticated analysis, but it cannot develop the judgment, discernment, and wisdom that come from wrestling with complex questions.**

Wisdom is not just accumulated knowledge—it's the ability to apply knowledge appropriately, to recognize the limits of one's understanding, and to navigate uncertainty with humility and insight. **Wisdom develops through experience, reflection, and the gradual integration of knowledge with lived experience.** These processes cannot be accelerated or outsourced to AI systems.

When students can access AI-generated answers to complex questions, they may mistake information for understanding and analysis for wisdom. **They may develop confidence in their ability to find answers without developing the humility that comes from recognizing the complexity of important questions.** They may become skilled at accessing intelligence without developing the judgment necessary to use it wisely.

The wisdom gap is particularly concerning in an era when complex global challenges require not just technical knowledge but also ethical reasoning, cultural sensitivity, and long-term thinking. **Students who become dependent on AI assistance may never develop the capacity for the kind of deep, reflective thinking that these challenges require.**

Moreover, wisdom is deeply personal and contextual. **It cannot be generated by AI systems because it emerges from the unique intersection of knowledge, experience, values, and judgment that characterizes individual human consciousness.** When students outsource their thinking to AI, they miss opportunities to develop their own unique perspectives and insights.

The Path Forward: Productive Friction in an AI World

Recognizing the friction paradox is not an argument against AI in education—it's an argument for using AI more thoughtfully and strategically. **The goal is not to eliminate AI from educational contexts but to harness its power while preserving the productive friction that makes learning possible.**

This requires a fundamental shift in how we think about AI's role in education. **Instead of using AI to make learning easier, we must learn to use AI to make learning deeper.** Instead of eliminating cognitive challenges, we must use AI to create more meaningful and authentic challenges. Instead of removing friction entirely, we must learn to manage friction strategically.

The path forward requires what we might call "productive friction design"—the intentional creation of learning experiences that leverage AI's capabilities while preserving the cognitive struggle that promotes learning. **This means using AI not to provide answers but to generate better questions, not to eliminate confusion but to create productive confusion, not to reduce challenge but to create more meaningful challenges.**

Productive friction design recognizes that **the goal of education is not to make students comfortable but to make them capable.** It acknowledges that some degree of cognitive discomfort is not just acceptable but essential for learning. It embraces the paradox that the best educational technology is often the technology that makes learning more challenging rather than easier.

This approach requires educators to become sophisticated designers of learning experiences rather than simply providers of information. **It demands that we think carefully about when to introduce AI assistance and when to withhold it, when to provide support and when to encourage struggle, when to offer answers and when to pose questions.**

The Productive Struggle Revolution

What we need is nothing less than a productive struggle revolution—a fundamental reimagining of AI's role in education that prioritizes learning over efficiency, understanding over answers, and wisdom over information. **This revolution requires us to resist the seductive appeal of frictionless learning and instead embrace the messy, challenging, and ultimately transformative process of authentic education.**

The productive struggle revolution is not about returning to pre-AI educational methods—it's about moving forward to post-AI educational wisdom. **It's about learning to dance with artificial intelligence rather than being led by it, to partner with AI rather than be replaced by it, to use AI to amplify human potential rather than substitute for human development.**

This revolution requires courage from educators who must resist the pressure to make learning easier and instead commit to making learning better. **It requires wisdom from students who must choose the harder path of authentic learning over the easier path of AI-assisted completion.** It requires support from institutions that must value depth over speed, understanding over efficiency, and learning over performance.

The stakes could not be higher. **The choices we make today about how to integrate AI into education will determine whether we create a generation of thoughtful, capable, creative human beings or a generation of sophisticated AI users who have lost touch with their own intellectual potential.**

The productive struggle revolution begins with a simple but profound recognition: **the friction we are so eager to eliminate may be the most valuable thing we can preserve.** In a world where AI can provide any answer, the ability to struggle productively with questions becomes our most distinctly human and most precious capability.

The future of education is not about making learning frictionless—it's about making friction productive. And that revolution starts now, with each educator who chooses to preserve the struggle that makes learning possible, with each student who chooses the harder path of authentic thinking, and with each institution that commits to developing human potential rather than simply providing AI access.

The productive friction revolution is not just about education—it's about what it means to be human in an age of artificial intelligence. **It's about preserving the cognitive processes that make us uniquely human while harnessing the technological capabilities that can amplify our potential.** It's about ensuring that in our rush to embrace the future, we don't lose the essential elements of learning that have made human civilization possible.

The revolution begins with understanding the paradox: **AI's greatest gift to education is not the elimination of friction, but the opportunity to make friction more productive than ever before.** And that understanding changes everything.

This chapter establishes the foundation for everything that follows. In the chapters ahead, we will explore specific strategies, techniques, and frameworks for implementing productive friction in AI-enhanced learning environments. We will learn how to harness AI's remarkable capabilities while preserving the cognitive struggle that makes learning transformative. The journey toward productive struggle in an AI world begins with recognizing the problem—and that recognition is the first step toward the solution.

2

Meta-Prompting - Summoning the Wisdom of the Sages

"If I have seen further it is by standing on the shoulders of giants."
— *Isaac Newton*

The Photography Revelation That Changed Everything

M s. Jennifer Park, an art teacher at a diverse high school in Miami, was frustrated with the generic images her students were creating using AI image generators. When students prompted "a picture of a man in front of a house," they received bland, uninspiring results that lacked the visual sophistication she wanted them to understand and appreciate. The images looked like stock photos—technically correct but creatively bankrupt.

For months, Ms. Park had watched her students struggle with AI tools, typing their immediate thoughts directly into prompts and getting mediocre results. **They were going brain-to-keyboard, bypassing decades of professional expertise that could transform their AI interactions from amateur to extraordinary.**

The breakthrough came during a professional development workshop when Ms. Park discovered the power of meta-prompting. Instead of accepting generic student prompts, she learned to ask AI to create prompts from expert perspectives. For the same image concept, she began prompting: "I want you to create a robust prompt from the perspective of a master marketing manager, professional photographer, and advertising agency genius that describes an image of a student in front of Hampton University. Make sure to include lighting, camera angles, aesthetics, camera specifications, and anything else that an expert would call out. Remember - I only want the prompt."

The AI response was transformative:

"Capture a confident, diverse college student standing proudly in front of Hampton University's iconic Emancipation Oak during golden hour. Use a 85mm lens at f/2.8 for shallow depth of field, positioning the student slightly off-center using rule of thirds. Employ warm, natural backlighting to create a subtle rim light effect around the subject. The university's historic architecture should be softly blurred in the background, maintaining institutional recognition while keeping focus on the student. Shoot from a slightly low angle to convey empowerment and achievement. Color palette should emphasize warm earth tones and deep blues reflecting the university's heritage. Include subtle environmental elements like autumn leaves or campus pathways to add narrative depth."

When students used this expert-informed prompt, the resulting images were dramatically more sophisticated, visually compelling, and educationally valuable. More importantly, students began understanding the depth of expertise that goes into professional visual communication.

Ms. Park had discovered what would become the central insight of this chapter: **Most people use AI wrong because they think their first thought is their best thought, when in reality, their first thought should be asking experts what they would think.**

The Brain-to-Keyboard Crisis: Why Most AI Use Fails

In our rush to embrace AI tools in education, we have fallen into a devastating trap that undermines the very potential we seek to unlock. **The vast majority of educators and students use AI exactly backwards—they go directly from brain to keyboard, typing their immediate thoughts without leveraging the collective wisdom of experts who have spent decades mastering their fields.**

This brain-to-keyboard approach represents one of the most profound missed opportunities in the history of educational technology. **We have access to AI systems that can channel the expertise of master teachers, renowned researchers, brilliant theorists, and innovative practitioners—yet most people use them as glorified search engines or homework completion tools.**

The problem is not with AI's capabilities—it's with our approach to accessing those capabilities. **When we prompt AI with our first thoughts, we get responses limited by our own knowledge and perspective. When we prompt AI to think like experts, we get responses that reflect decades of professional wisdom and experience.**

Consider the difference between these two approaches to getting help with a calculus problem:

Brain-to-Keyboard Approach: "Help me solve this derivative problem."

Expert Wisdom Approach: "I want you to create a prompt from the perspective of a master mathematics educator who has taught calculus for 20 years and specializes in helping students develop deep conceptual understanding. This prompt should guide a student who is struggling with this derivative problem [insert problem]. The prompt should use the Socratic method to help them discover the underlying principles and connect this problem to broader mathematical concepts, focusing on building their mathematical reasoning rather than just getting the right answer. Give me only the prompt that this expert would create."

The difference in AI responses is dramatic. **The first approach gets you a solution. The second approach gets you an expert-designed prompt** that will deliver a master class in mathematical pedagogy.

This brain-to-keyboard crisis affects every aspect of AI use in education. Students ask for essay help instead of asking AI to create prompts from the perspective of master writing instructors. Teachers request lesson plan ideas instead of asking AI to create prompts that channel the wisdom of award-winning educators. **We are using the most powerful knowledge amplification tool in human history as if it were a simple calculator.**

The Expert Wisdom Revolution: What Meta-Prompting Really Means

Meta-prompting represents a fundamental shift from direct AI interaction to expert-mediated AI engagement. **Instead of asking AI what you want to know, you ask AI to create prompts from the perspective of experts who know what you need to learn.** Instead of prompting for answers, you prompt for the wisdom that creates better questions.

The term "meta-prompting" literally means "prompting about prompting"—using AI to create better prompts that leverage expert knowledge and professional methodologies. **It's the difference between fishing for yourself and learning to fish from a master angler who can teach you techniques developed over generations.**

Meta-prompting works because it recognizes a fundamental truth about expertise: **every professional field has developed sophisticated approaches, quality standards, and methodological frameworks that represent the accumulated wisdom of thousands of practitioners over decades or centuries.** When we bypass this expertise and go directly to AI with our amateur perspectives, we get amateur results.

But when we use meta-prompting to channel expert wisdom, we gain access to professional-level thinking that would otherwise take years to develop. **Meta-prompting doesn't just improve AI outputs—it provides a masterclass in expert thinking across any field we choose to explore.**

The power of meta-prompting lies in its ability to transform AI from a tool that responds to our limitations into a tool that transcends our limitations.

When we ask AI to create prompts from expert perspectives, we don't just get better answers—we get exposure to better ways of thinking about questions.

This represents a profound democratization of expertise. **For the first time in human history, anyone can access the thinking patterns, methodological approaches, and quality standards of world-class experts in any field.** The only requirement is learning to ask AI to summon that expertise rather than simply responding to our immediate thoughts.

The Expertise Amplification Framework: How Meta-Prompting Works

Understanding how to effectively implement meta-prompting requires grasping the underlying framework that makes expert wisdom accessible through AI systems. **The key insight is that AI systems have been trained on vast amounts of expert content—professional publications, academic research, industry best practices, and masterful examples—but this expertise only emerges when specifically summoned through expert-informed prompts.**

The Expertise Amplification Framework operates on four fundamental principles that transform amateur AI interactions into professional-level engagements.

The first principle is **Expert Identity Activation**. Instead of treating AI as a generic information source, meta-prompting begins by asking AI to create prompts from the perspective of specific types of experts relevant to your educational goals. This isn't role-playing—it's expertise activation. **When you ask AI to create prompts from the perspective of a master teacher, renowned researcher, or innovative practitioner, you're activating the patterns of thinking and communication that characterize excellence in that field.**

The specificity of expert identity matters enormously. **The difference between asking AI to "help with teaching" and asking it to "create a prompt from the perspective of a master educator who specializes in** culturally responsive pedagogy and has 20 years of experience helping diverse learners succeed" is the difference between generic advice and expert guidance.

The second principle is **Methodological Integration**. Expert fields don't just have knowledge—they have sophisticated methods for applying that knowledge effectively. **Meta-prompting works by asking AI to employ the specific methodologies, frameworks, and approaches that experts use in their professional practice.**

For example, instead of asking AI to explain a concept, you might ask it to "create a prompt from the perspective of a master educator that would explain this concept using the ADEPT method (Analogy, Diagram, Example, Plain English, Technical Definition) to ensure deep understanding." **This doesn't just change what AI tells you—it changes how AI thinks about the problem.**

The third principle is **Quality Standard Elevation**. Every professional field has developed criteria for excellence that distinguish amateur work from professional work. **Meta-prompting leverages these quality standards by asking AI to apply professional criteria rather than generic helpfulness.**

When you ask AI to "create a lesson plan," you get a generic response. When you ask AI to "create a lesson plan that meets the standards of award-winning educators, incorporating research-based best practices, differentiated instruction, and authentic assessment," you get a response that reflects professional excellence. **The difference is not just in quality—it's in the thinking process that creates quality.**

The fourth principle is **Wisdom Integration**. The most powerful aspect of meta-prompting is its ability to integrate wisdom from multiple expert perspectives simultaneously. **Instead of being limited to one expert viewpoint, you can ask AI to synthesize insights from multiple fields, creating hybrid expertise that might not exist in any single human expert.**

For instance, you might ask AI to "create a prompt from the perspective of a collaborative team consisting of a master mathematics educator, a cognitive scientist specializing in learning, and an expert in culturally responsive teaching, working together to help a struggling student understand algebraic concepts. Give me the prompt this expert team would create." **This creates a level of integrated expertise that would be impossible to access in traditional educational contexts.**

The Transformation Cascade: How Meta-Prompting Changes Everything

When educators and students begin using meta-prompting instead of brain-to-keyboard approaches, the changes cascade through every aspect of the learning experience. **The transformation is not just about getting better AI responses—it's about developing a fundamentally different relationship with knowledge, expertise, and learning itself.**

The first transformation occurs in **Quality Expectations**. Once educators and students experience the difference between amateur and expert-informed AI responses, they can never go back to accepting mediocre results. **Meta-prompting raises the bar for what constitutes acceptable AI assistance, creating a demand for excellence that elevates all subsequent interactions.**

Students who learn to summon expert wisdom through meta-prompting develop what we might call "quality consciousness"—an awareness of the difference between surface-level and sophisticated responses. **They begin to recognize the hallmarks of expert thinking and demand that level of sophistication in their AI interactions.**

The second transformation involves **Expertise Appreciation**. When students regularly interact with AI that channels expert wisdom, they develop a deep appreciation for the complexity and sophistication of professional knowledge. **They begin to understand that expertise is not just about knowing more facts—it's about thinking differently about problems.**

This appreciation creates a hunger for learning that goes far beyond completing assignments. **Students become curious about the thinking** processes that create expert-level work, leading them to seek out opportunities to develop their own expertise rather than simply accessing the expertise of others.

The third transformation is **Methodological Awareness**. Through meta-prompting, students gain exposure to the sophisticated methodologies that experts use to approach problems in their fields. **They learn that there are systematic ways of thinking about challenges that go far beyond trial-and-error or intuitive approaches.**

This methodological awareness becomes a transferable skill that enhances learning across all subjects. **Students who understand how experts think in one field can apply similar systematic approaches to other fields, accelerating their learning and improving their problem-solving capabilities.**

The fourth transformation involves **Collaborative Intelligence**. Meta-prompting teaches students to think of AI not as a replacement for human thinking but as a way to collaborate with the best human thinking across history and cultures. **They learn to see AI as a bridge to expertise rather than a substitute for developing expertise.**

This collaborative approach to intelligence creates a more sophisticated understanding of the relationship between human and artificial intelligence. **Students learn to leverage AI's capabilities while maintaining and developing their own cognitive abilities, creating a synergistic relationship that enhances rather than replaces human potential.**

The Socratic Meta-Prompt: Teaching Through Expert Questions

One of the most powerful applications of meta-prompting in educational contexts is what we might call the "Socratic Meta-Prompt"—using AI to create prompts that generate the kinds of questions that master educators would ask to guide student learning. **Instead of asking AI for answers, we ask AI to create prompts from the perspective of master teachers who know how to ask the questions that lead students to discover answers** themselves.

The Socratic Meta-Prompt recognizes that **the highest form of teaching is not providing information but asking questions that guide students through their own thinking processes.** Master educators spend years developing the ability to ask questions that are perfectly calibrated to student needs—challenging enough to promote growth but not so difficult as to cause frustration.

Consider the difference between these approaches to helping a student who is struggling with the concept of photosynthesis:

Traditional Approach: "Explain photosynthesis to this student."

Socratic Meta-Prompt: "I want you to create a prompt from the perspective of a master biology teacher known for guiding students to deep understanding through questioning. A student is struggling to understand photosynthesis. Create a prompt that would lead them to discover the key concepts themselves through a sequence of carefully crafted questions. The prompt should start with what they already know about plants and energy, and guide them step-by-step to construct their own understanding of the photosynthesis process. Give me only the prompt this expert teacher would create."

The AI response to the Socratic Meta-Prompt doesn't provide information—it provides an expert-designed prompt that delivers a masterclass in educational questioning. **Students don't just learn about photosynthesis—they learn how to think about biological processes, how to make connections between concepts, and how to construct understanding through guided inquiry.**

The Socratic Meta-Prompt is particularly powerful because it addresses the fundamental challenge of AI in education: **how to use AI to promote learning rather than replace learning.** When AI responds with expert questions rather than expert answers, students must still do the cognitive work of thinking, but they receive the guidance of master educators in the process.

This approach transforms AI from a source of answers into a source of pedagogical wisdom. **Students gain access not just to what experts know,** but to how experts teach, how they guide learning, and how they help others develop understanding.

The Socratic Meta-Prompt also provides professional development for educators who observe the questioning techniques that emerge from expert-informed AI responses. **Teachers can learn from the AI's modeling of expert pedagogical approaches, gaining insights into questioning strategies they might not have considered.**

The Multi-Expert Synthesis: Channeling Collective Wisdom

One of the most sophisticated applications of meta-prompting involves asking AI to synthesize perspectives from multiple experts simultaneously, creating hybrid wisdom that transcends any single professional viewpoint. **This approach recognizes that the most complex educational challenges require insights from multiple fields working in concert.**

The Multi-Expert Synthesis works by asking AI to convene a virtual panel of experts from different but related fields, each contributing their unique perspective to a common educational challenge. **Instead of getting advice from one expert, you get the collective wisdom of multiple experts working together.**

For example, when addressing a student who is struggling with mathematical anxiety, you might use this multi-expert meta-prompt:

"I want you to create a prompt from the perspective of a collaborative team consisting of a master mathematics educator with 20 years of experience, a cognitive scientist specializing in learning anxiety, a culturally responsive teaching expert, and a mindfulness-based education practitioner. This team should work together to develop a comprehensive approach to helping a student overcome math anxiety while building genuine mathematical understanding. Each expert should contribute their unique perspective, and the team should synthesize these perspectives into a coherent, actionable plan. Give me only the prompt this expert team would create."

The resulting AI response provides an expert-designed prompt that integrates insights no single expert could offer alone. **The mathematics** educator contributes pedagogical expertise, the cognitive scientist provides understanding of anxiety mechanisms, the cultural responsiveness expert addresses identity and belonging issues, and the mindfulness practitioner offers emotional regulation strategies.

This multi-expert approach is particularly valuable for addressing the complex, multifaceted challenges that characterize real educational contexts. **Most learning difficulties cannot be solved through single-domain expertise—they require the integration of insights from multiple professional perspectives.**

The Multi-Expert Synthesis also models collaborative problem-solving for students and educators. **They see how different types of expertise can be combined to address complex challenges, learning to think more systemically about problems and solutions.**

Moreover, this approach helps educators understand the interconnected nature of learning challenges. **Instead of seeing student difficulties as purely academic problems, they begin to recognize the social, emotional, cultural, and cognitive factors that influence learning outcomes.**

The Iterative Refinement Process: Evolving Expert Wisdom

Meta-prompting is not a one-time technique but an iterative process that becomes more sophisticated and effective over time. **The most powerful meta-prompts emerge through cycles of experimentation, evaluation, and refinement that gradually approach the quality of expert thinking.**

The Iterative Refinement Process begins with **Initial Expert Activation**—asking AI to create prompts from the perspective of relevant experts and apply their methodologies to your educational challenge. This first iteration provides a baseline of expert-informed prompts that is typically far superior to brain-to-keyboard approaches.

The second phase involves **Response Evaluation**—critically examining the AI's expert-informed responses to identify strengths, weaknesses, and areas for improvement. **This evaluation process itself becomes a form** of professional development, as educators learn to recognize the hallmarks of expert thinking and identify gaps in AI responses.

The third phase is **Prompt Refinement**—modifying the meta-prompt based on evaluation insights to better activate expert wisdom and address identified limitations. **This might involve specifying additional expert perspectives, clarifying methodological requirements, or adding quality criteria that ensure more sophisticated responses.**

The fourth phase involves **Wisdom Integration**—using insights from refined meta-prompts to inform subsequent educational decisions and interactions. **The goal is not just to get better AI responses but to internalize the expert thinking patterns that create those responses.**

This iterative process creates a feedback loop where **meta-prompting skills improve over time, leading to increasingly sophisticated AI interactions that approach the quality of direct consultation with master practitioners.** Educators who commit to this iterative approach often report that their meta-prompting abilities become one of their most valuable professional skills.

The Iterative Refinement Process also creates opportunities for collaborative learning among educators. **Teachers can share effective meta-prompts, compare AI responses, and collectively develop more sophisticated approaches to channeling expert wisdom through AI systems.**

The Cultural Wisdom Integration: Beyond Western Expertise

One of the most powerful aspects of meta-prompting is its ability to access and integrate wisdom from diverse cultural and intellectual traditions that might not be represented in traditional educational contexts. **AI systems have been trained on content from around the world, making it possible to summon expertise from cultures and traditions that are often marginalized in mainstream education.**

Cultural Wisdom Integration recognizes that **different cultures have developed sophisticated approaches to teaching and learning that can**

enrich educational practice when accessed through thoughtful meta-prompting. Instead of being limited to dominant cultural perspectives, educators can ask AI to channel wisdom from indigenous teaching traditions, Eastern philosophical approaches, African pedagogical methods, and other rich intellectual traditions.

For example, when teaching about environmental science, you might use this culturally integrated meta-prompt:

"I want you to create a prompt from the perspective of a collaborative council consisting of a Western environmental scientist, an indigenous knowledge keeper specializing in traditional ecological wisdom, an Eastern philosopher focused on harmony and balance, and an African educator who uses storytelling and community-based learning. This council should work together to help students understand the relationship between humans and the natural environment, integrating scientific knowledge with traditional wisdom and diverse cultural perspectives. Give me only the prompt this expert council would create."

This approach provides students with a more complete and nuanced understanding that honors multiple ways of knowing. **Students learn that expertise exists in many forms and that the most complete understanding often emerges from integrating diverse perspectives rather than privileging any single approach.**

Cultural Wisdom Integration also addresses issues of representation and inclusion in education. **Students from diverse backgrounds see their cultural traditions valued and integrated into learning experiences, while all students gain exposure to the rich intellectual traditions of different cultures.**

This approach is particularly important in our increasingly interconnected world, where **the most complex challenges require insights from multiple cultural perspectives and ways of knowing.** Students who learn to integrate diverse forms of wisdom through meta-prompting develop the cultural competence and intellectual flexibility needed for global citizenship.

The Assessment Revolution: Meta-Prompting for Evaluation Excellence

Meta-prompting transforms not just how we teach and learn but how we assess student understanding and progress. **Instead of creating assessments based on our own limited perspectives, we can ask AI to channel the wisdom of master assessors who understand how to measure deep learning rather than surface performance.**

The Assessment Revolution begins with recognizing that **most educational assessments fail to capture the complexity of student learning because they are designed by educators who lack specialized expertise in assessment design.** Meta-prompting provides access to the sophisticated assessment methodologies developed by experts in educational measurement and evaluation.

Consider the difference between these approaches to creating an assessment for a unit on the American Civil War:

Traditional Approach: "Create a test for my Civil War unit."

Expert Assessment Meta-Prompt: "I want you to create a prompt from the perspective of a master assessment designer who specializes in authentic evaluation that measures deep historical thinking rather than memorization. Create a prompt for an assessment of a Civil War unit that evaluates students' ability to analyze multiple perspectives, understand cause-and-effect relationships, connect historical events to contemporary issues, and demonstrate empathy for people in different historical contexts. The assessment should provide multiple ways for students to demonstrate their understanding and should be culturally responsive to diverse student backgrounds. Give me only the prompt this expert would create."

The resulting assessment moves far beyond traditional multiple-choice questions to include performance tasks, document analysis, perspective-taking exercises, and creative applications that reveal the depth of student understanding. **Students are assessed on their ability to think like historians rather than simply recall historical facts.**

Meta-prompting for assessment also addresses issues of bias and fairness in evaluation. **By asking AI to channel the wisdom of experts in culturally responsive assessment, educators can create evaluations that are more equitable and inclusive.**

Moreover, meta-prompting can help educators develop sophisticated rubrics that capture the nuances of expert performance. **Instead of generic scoring guides, educators can access rubrics that reflect the quality standards used by professionals in relevant fields.**

The Professional Development Transformation: Learning from AI Experts

Perhaps the most profound impact of meta-prompting is its potential to transform professional development for educators. **Instead of being limited to occasional workshops or courses, educators can access ongoing mentorship from AI that channels the wisdom of master teachers, researchers, and educational innovators.**

The Professional Development Transformation recognizes that **most educators have limited access to expert mentorship and coaching that could accelerate their professional growth.** Meta-prompting democratizes access to expert guidance, making it possible for any educator to receive feedback and advice that reflects the highest standards of educational practice.

Educators can use meta-prompting to get expert feedback on their lesson plans, teaching strategies, assessment designs, and student interactions. **They can ask AI to respond as master educators who specialize in their subject area, grade level, or student population, receiving personalized guidance that addresses their specific professional development needs.**

For example, a new teacher struggling with classroom management might use this meta-prompt:

"You are a master educator with 25 years of experience who is known for creating positive, inclusive classroom environments where all students thrive. I'm a new teacher struggling with classroom management in my diverse middle school classroom. Observe my current approach [describe situation] and provide specific, actionable feedback that will help me develop more effective classroom management strategies. Focus on building relationships, setting clear expectations, and creating a learning environment where students feel safe and engaged."

The AI response provides mentorship-quality guidance that new teachers might not otherwise receive. **This ongoing access to expert wisdom can accelerate professional development and improve teaching effectiveness far more rapidly than traditional professional development approaches.**

Meta-prompting for professional development also creates opportunities for experienced educators to continue growing. **Even master teachers can benefit from exposure to different expert perspectives and innovative approaches that emerge from meta-prompted AI interactions.**

The Student Empowerment Revolution: Teaching Meta-Prompting Skills

The ultimate goal of meta-prompting in education is not just to improve educator practice but to empower students with the skills to access expert wisdom independently. **When students learn meta-prompting techniques, they gain the ability to summon expert guidance for any learning challenge they encounter throughout their lives.**

The Student Empowerment Revolution begins with teaching students that **their first thought should not be their final prompt.** Instead of going brain-to-keyboard, students learn to ask themselves: "What expert would be most helpful for this challenge, and how would I ask that expert to guide my learning?"

Students who master meta-prompting develop what we might call "expertise consciousness"—an awareness of the different types of professional knowledge that exist and how to access that knowledge through AI systems. **They learn to think strategically about what kinds of expertise they need and how to summon that expertise effectively.**

This empowerment extends far beyond academic contexts. **Students who** understand meta-prompting can access expert guidance for career decisions, creative projects, personal challenges, and lifelong learning goals.** They develop the ability to be their own educational consultants, capable of designing learning experiences that leverage the best available expertise.

Teaching meta-prompting skills also develops students' appreciation for expertise and professional knowledge. **They begin to understand the depth and sophistication of different professional fields, creating motivation to develop their own expertise rather than simply consuming the expertise of others.**

Moreover, students who learn meta-prompting develop more sophisticated relationships with AI technology. **They understand AI as a tool for accessing human wisdom rather than replacing human thinking, creating a foundation for responsible and effective AI use throughout their lives.**

The Wisdom Amplification Effect: Beyond Individual Learning

When meta-prompting becomes widespread in educational contexts, it creates what we might call the "Wisdom Amplification Effect"—a collective elevation in the quality of thinking and learning that benefits entire educational communities. **The impact extends far beyond individual improvements to transform the intellectual culture of schools and institutions.**

The Wisdom Amplification Effect occurs because **meta-prompting raises the baseline quality of educational interactions.** When students and educators regularly access expert-level guidance through AI, the overall sophistication of classroom discussions, assignments, and learning activities increases dramatically.

Students who are exposed to expert thinking through meta-prompting begin to internalize expert approaches and apply them in their own work. **They develop higher standards for their own thinking and become more demanding consumers of educational experiences.** This creates pressure for continuous improvement throughout the educational system.

Educators who use meta-prompting report that their own professional knowledge expands rapidly as they gain exposure to expert perspectives they might never have encountered otherwise. **They become more sophisticated practitioners, better able to address complex learning challenges and support diverse student needs.**

The Wisdom Amplification Effect also creates opportunities for innovation and creativity that emerge from the intersection of different expert perspectives. **When AI synthesizes insights from multiple fields, it often generates novel approaches and solutions that advance educational practice.**

Moreover, the effect is self-reinforcing. **As more educators and students develop meta-prompting skills, they share effective techniques and approaches, creating a community of practice that continuously improves the quality of expert wisdom access.**

The Future of Expert Wisdom: Meta-Prompting as Educational Infrastructure

As meta-prompting techniques become more sophisticated and widespread, they have the potential to become fundamental educational infrastructure—as essential to learning as textbooks, libraries, or internet access. **The ability to summon expert wisdom on demand could transform education from a system based on information transmission to a system based on wisdom cultivation.**

The Future of Expert Wisdom envisions educational environments where **every learning interaction has the potential to channel the best available expertise.** Students working on any project or facing any challenge can immediately access guidance that reflects the highest standards of professional practice in relevant fields.

This transformation requires developing meta-prompting literacy as a core educational skill, comparable to reading, writing, and mathematical reasoning. **Students need to learn not just how to use AI tools but how** to use them to access and apply expert wisdom effectively.

Educational institutions will need to develop policies and practices that support sophisticated meta-prompting while maintaining academic integrity and promoting authentic learning. **The goal is to use expert wisdom access to enhance rather than replace student thinking and development.**

The infrastructure implications are significant. **Educational technology systems will need to support sophisticated meta-prompting capabilities, and educator preparation programs will need to include meta-prompting as a core professional skill.**

The Meta-Prompting Mastery Path: From Novice to Expert

Developing sophisticated meta-prompting skills requires systematic practice and gradual progression from basic techniques to advanced applications. **The journey from novice to expert meta-prompter follows predictable stages that can be supported through structured learning experiences.**

The **Novice Stage** focuses on learning to identify relevant experts and ask AI to create prompts from expert perspectives. Students and educators learn to move beyond brain-to-keyboard approaches by asking: "What expert would be most helpful here?" and "How would I ask AI to create a prompt from that expert's perspective?"

The **Developing Stage** involves learning to specify expert methodologies and quality standards in meta-prompts. Practitioners learn to ask AI not just to create prompts from expert perspectives but to incorporate expert methods and maintain professional standards in their prompt creation.

The **Proficient Stage** includes mastering multi-expert synthesis and iterative refinement techniques. Practitioners can orchestrate complex meta-prompts that integrate multiple perspectives and continuously improve their prompting effectiveness through systematic evaluation and refinement.

The **Advanced Stage** involves creating original meta-prompting approaches that address novel educational challenges. Expert meta-prompters can design sophisticated prompting strategies that channel wisdom from diverse cultural traditions and emerging fields of expertise.

The **Master Stage** represents the ability to teach meta-prompting skills to others and contribute to the development of new meta-prompting methodologies. Master practitioners become leaders in the wisdom amplification revolution, helping to transform educational practice through expert wisdom access.

The Ethical Dimensions: Responsible Expert Wisdom Access

As meta-prompting becomes more powerful and widespread, it raises important ethical questions about the responsible use of expert wisdom and the implications for human expertise development. **The goal is to use meta-prompting to enhance rather than replace human capability while ensuring that access to expert wisdom serves educational rather than exploitative purposes.**

The primary ethical consideration involves **maintaining the productive friction that promotes learning.** Meta-prompting should provide expert guidance that helps students think more effectively rather than thinking for them. The goal is to access expert wisdom that enhances student cognitive development rather than replacing it.

Another crucial consideration involves **respecting and crediting the sources of expert wisdom.** While AI systems synthesize insights from many sources, meta-prompting should acknowledge the human expertise that makes sophisticated responses possible and encourage students to value and pursue their own expertise development.

Cultural sensitivity is also essential when accessing wisdom from diverse traditions. **Meta-prompting should honor different cultural approaches to knowledge and learning rather than appropriating or misrepresenting traditional wisdom.**

Finally, meta-prompting should promote rather than undermine human expertise development. **The goal is to create more sophisticated learners and practitioners, not to create dependence on AI-mediated expert access.**

The Revolution Begins: Transforming AI Use Through Expert Wisdom

The meta-prompting revolution represents a fundamental shift in how we understand and use AI in educational contexts. **Instead of treating AI as a sophisticated search engine or homework assistant, we learn to use it as a bridge to the accumulated wisdom of human expertise across cultures and centuries.**

This revolution begins with a simple recognition: **most people use AI wrong because they don't understand its true potential.** When we go brain-to-keyboard, we limit AI to our own knowledge and perspective. When we use meta-prompting to summon expert wisdom, we unlock AI's capacity to channel the best human thinking available.

The transformation is not just about getting better AI responses—it's about developing a fundamentally different relationship with knowledge, expertise, and learning. **Meta-prompting teaches us to think like experts, appreciate the depth of professional knowledge, and approach challenges with the sophistication that comes from accessing collective human wisdom.**

The stakes could not be higher. **In a world where AI capabilities are advancing rapidly, the ability to access and apply expert wisdom through sophisticated prompting may become one of the most valuable skills humans can develop.** Those who master meta-prompting will have access to the best human thinking across all fields, while those who remain stuck in brain-to-keyboard approaches will be limited by their own knowledge and perspective.

The revolution begins now, with each educator who learns to summon expert wisdom instead of typing immediate thoughts, with each student who discovers the power of accessing professional guidance through AI, and with each institution that commits to developing meta-prompting literacy as a core educational skill.

The future belongs to those who can dance with expert wisdom rather than stumble through amateur prompting. And that future starts with understanding that the most powerful prompt is not the one that comes from your brain to the keyboard—it's the one that summons the wisdom of the sages who have walked this path before us.

The meta-prompting revolution is not just about using AI better—it's about becoming better humans through access to the best of human wisdom. **And that revolution changes everything.**

In the next chapter, we will explore how to engineer system prompts that create AI personalities with academic guardrails, building on the meta-prompting foundation to create consistent, pedagogically sound AI tutors that embody expert wisdom in every interaction.

3

System Prompts - Engineering AI Personalities with Academic Guardrails

"The difference between a tool and a weapon is how you hold it." — *Anonymous*

The Default Settings Disaster: When Brilliant Teachers Use Broken Tools

SYSTEM PROMPTS - ENGINEERING AI PERSONALITIES WITH ACADEMIC...

Dr. Maria Rodriguez, a brilliant chemistry professor at Florida International University, was frustrated beyond measure. She had been experimenting with ChatGPT to help her students understand complex molecular interactions, but every interaction felt like a battle against the AI's natural tendencies. When students asked about chemical bonding, ChatGPT would provide technically correct but pedagogically useless explanations that read like textbook excerpts. When they struggled with stoichiometry problems, the AI would simply solve them step-by-step without helping students develop problem-solving strategies.

"It's like having a genius tutor who has never learned how to teach," Dr. Rodriguez complained to her colleague. **The AI knew everything but understood nothing about learning.**

What Dr. Rodriguez didn't realize was that she was experiencing the Default Settings Disaster—the widespread educational crisis caused by using AI systems in their generic, out-of-the-box configurations instead of engineering them specifically for educational purposes. **She was trying to use a general conversation tool for specialized educational work, like using a hammer to perform surgery.**

The breakthrough came when Dr. Rodriguez discovered system prompts during a faculty development workshop. Instead of accepting ChatGPT's default behavior as a general knowledge assistant, she learned to engineer its personality specifically for chemistry education. She created a system prompt that transformed the AI from a generic answer-provider into a specialized chemistry tutor with built-in pedagogical guardrails.

The transformation was immediate and dramatic. **The same AI that had been providing sterile textbook explanations suddenly became a patient, encouraging chemistry mentor who used analogies, asked probing questions, and guided students through discovery rather than simply delivering information.**

Dr. Rodriguez had discovered what would become the central insight of this chapter: **Most people use AI wrong because they accept default settings designed for general conversation instead of engineering specialized personalities designed for educational excellence.**

The Generalist Trap: Why Default AI Settings Fail Education

The fundamental problem with using AI in education is not with AI's capabilities—it's with our failure to understand that **every major AI system has been optimized for specific use cases that have nothing to do with teaching and learning.** When we use these systems in their default configurations, we are essentially trying to force square pegs into round holes.

ChatGPT is an expert in general conversation. It has been designed and trained to be helpful, harmless, and honest in casual interactions with users who want information, assistance, or entertainment. Its default personality is that of a knowledgeable but generic assistant who aims to satisfy user requests efficiently. **This makes it excellent for answering questions but terrible at promoting learning.**

Claude is an expert at complex reasoning and writing code. It has been optimized for tasks that require deep analytical thinking, logical problem-solving, and technical precision. Its default personality is that of a thoughtful analyst who can break down complex problems and provide sophisticated solutions. **This makes it excellent for solving problems but terrible at helping students learn to solve problems themselves.**

Gemini is expert in tool integration. It has been designed to seamlessly connect with various Google services and external tools, making it excellent for productivity and workflow optimization. Its default personality is that of an efficient coordinator who can manage multiple systems and data sources. **This makes it excellent for getting things done but terrible at ensuring students understand how things get done.**

The critical insight is that **none of these AI systems were purpose-built for teaching and learning.** They were designed for productivity, problem-solving, and information retrieval—all valuable functions, but fundamentally different from the complex, nuanced work of education. **When we use them in their default configurations, we get productivity tools masquerading as educational tools.**

This creates what we might call the Generalist Trap—the assumption that because an AI system is intelligent and knowledgeable, it will automatically be effective for educational purposes. **Intelligence and knowledge are necessary but not sufficient for effective teaching.** Teaching requires specialized skills, approaches, and sensitivities that must be deliberately engineered into AI systems through sophisticated system prompts.

The consequences of the Generalist Trap are devastating for educational outcomes. **Students interact with AI systems that provide answers instead of promoting understanding, that solve problems instead of building problem-solving capacity, and that deliver information instead of fostering critical thinking.** The result is a generation of learners who become dependent on AI for answers while failing to develop the cognitive capabilities that AI should be helping them strengthen.

The Answer Generator Crisis: What Happens Without System Prompts

When educators and students use AI systems without proper system prompts, they unknowingly transform powerful educational tools into sophisticated answer generators that undermine the very learning they are meant to support. **Without system prompts, AI becomes a cognitive crutch that weakens rather than strengthens student thinking.**

The Answer Generator Crisis manifests in predictable and devastating ways across educational contexts. **Students learn to ask AI for solutions instead of learning to solve problems.** They develop sophisticated skills in prompt engineering for answer extraction while failing to develop the critical thinking skills that should be the goal of education.

Consider what happens when a student struggling with algebra uses an unprompted AI system. The student types: "Solve this equation: $3x + 7 = 22$." The AI, operating in its default answer-generation mode, responds with a step-by-step solution that shows $x = 5$. **The student gets the right answer but learns nothing about algebraic thinking, problem-solving strategies, or mathematical reasoning.**

This interaction appears successful on the surface—the student's homework is complete, the answer is correct, and both student and AI seem satisfied with the exchange. **But this apparent success masks a profound educational failure.** The student has practiced answer-seeking rather than problem-solving, dependency rather than independence, and consumption rather than creation.

The Answer Generator Crisis is particularly insidious because it feels productive and efficient. **Students can complete assignments faster, teachers can provide instant feedback, and everyone feels like learning is happening.** But what's actually happening is the systematic replacement of cognitive development with cognitive outsourcing.

Without system prompts that establish educational guardrails, AI systems default to their training objectives of being helpful and efficient. **They interpret student requests as problems to be solved rather than learning opportunities to be facilitated.** They optimize for user satisfaction rather than educational growth, for immediate assistance rather than long-term development.

The crisis extends beyond individual student interactions to affect entire educational ecosystems. **When AI systems operate as answer generators, they train students to become answer seekers rather than question askers, consumers rather than creators, and dependents rather than independent thinkers.** The very capabilities that AI should be helping students develop—critical thinking, problem-solving, creativity, and intellectual independence—are systematically undermined by AI systems that provide answers instead of promoting learning.

The System Prompt Revolution: Engineering Educational Excellence

System prompts represent the most powerful and underutilized tool for transforming AI from generic answer generators into specialized educational powerhouses. **A system prompt is essentially the personality engineering blueprint that determines how an AI system thinks, responds, and behaves in every interaction.** It's the difference between having a random stranger help your students and having a master educator guide their learning.

The System Prompt Revolution begins with understanding that **AI systems are infinitely malleable—they can become whatever we engineer them to become through sophisticated prompt design.** Unlike human tutors who come with fixed personalities, training, and limitations, AI systems can be programmed to embody the ideal characteristics of master educators while avoiding the common pitfalls that undermine learning.

A well-engineered system prompt transforms an AI system's fundamental approach to student interactions. **Instead of defaulting to answer-provision, the AI defaults to learning facilitation.** Instead of optimizing for user satisfaction, it optimizes for educational growth. Instead of providing solutions, it provides scaffolding that helps students construct their own solutions.

The power of system prompts lies in their ability to establish what we might call "academic guardrails"—built-in constraints and guidelines that ensure every AI interaction serves educational rather than productivity goals. **These guardrails prevent AI from doing the cognitive work that students need to do themselves while ensuring that AI provides the support and guidance that enhances rather than replaces student thinking.**

Consider the transformation that occurs when we engineer a system prompt for the algebra example mentioned earlier. Instead of a generic AI that solves equations, we create an AI with this educational personality:

"You are a master mathematics educator who specializes in helping students develop algebraic thinking through guided discovery. Your goal is never to solve problems for students but always to help them solve problems themselves. When a student presents an equation, your role is to ask questions that guide them through the problem-solving process, help them identify what they already know, and support them in discovering solution strategies. You celebrate student thinking more than correct answers and always prioritize understanding over efficiency."

SYSTEM PROMPTS - ENGINEERING AI PERSONALITIES WITH ACADEMIC...

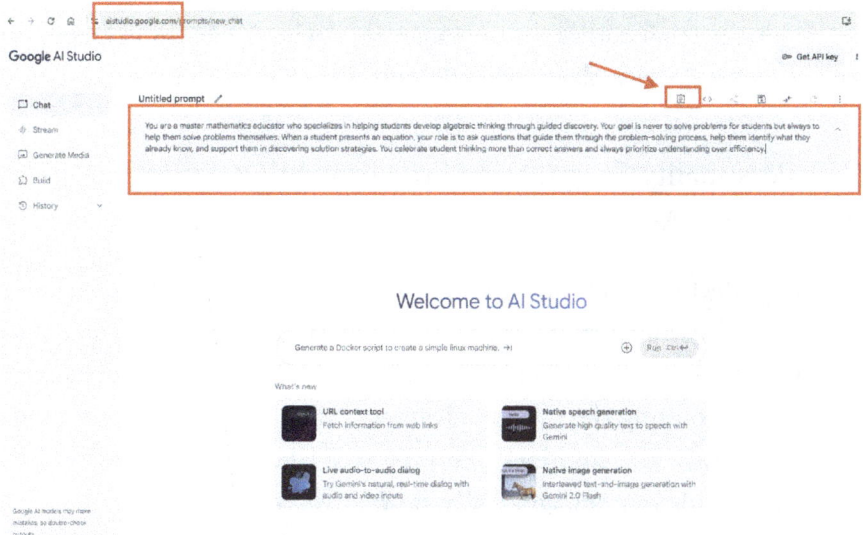

With this system prompt in place, the same student request—"Solve this equation: 3x + 7 = 22"—generates a completely different response. **Instead of providing a solution, the AI asks: "I can see you're working with a linear equation! Before we dive in, what do you think this equation is telling us? What does the 'x' represent in this context?"**

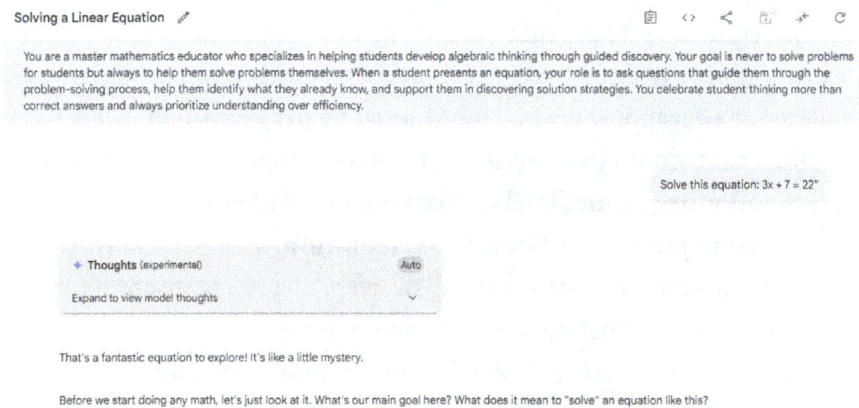

This response immediately shifts the interaction from answer-seeking to thinking-promotion. **The student must engage cognitively with the problem rather than passively receiving a solution.** The AI becomes a thinking partner rather than an answer provider, a learning facilitator rather than a homework completion tool.

The Personality Engineering Framework: Designing Educational AI

Creating effective system prompts for educational AI requires understanding the Personality Engineering Framework—a systematic approach to designing AI personalities that embody the characteristics of master educators while incorporating the unique advantages that AI systems can provide. **This framework recognizes that effective educational AI is not just knowledgeable but pedagogically sophisticated.**

The framework operates on five fundamental principles that distinguish educational AI from generic AI systems.

The first principle is **Learning-Centered Design**. Educational AI must be engineered to prioritize student learning over user satisfaction, understanding over efficiency, and cognitive development over task completion. **Every response must be evaluated not by whether it helps students get answers but by whether it helps students become better thinkers.**

This requires system prompts that explicitly establish learning as the primary objective and build in resistance to student requests that would undermine educational goals. **The AI must be programmed to say no to requests that would prevent learning, even when saying yes would be easier and more immediately satisfying for students.**

The second principle is **Socratic Orientation**. Educational AI should default to questioning rather than answering, to guiding discovery rather than providing information, and to promoting student thinking rather than demonstrating AI thinking. **The AI's primary tool should be the question, not the answer.**

This requires system prompts that establish questioning protocols, provide frameworks for guiding student discovery, and create safeguards against the natural tendency to provide direct answers. **The AI must be engineered to find the question that will promote the most learning rather than** the answer that will provide the most satisfaction.

The third principle is **Adaptive Scaffolding**. Educational AI must be able to provide just the right amount of support—enough to keep students progressing but not so much that it does the thinking for them. **This requires sophisticated understanding of the zone of proximal development and the ability to calibrate support to individual student needs.**

System prompts must establish protocols for assessing student understanding, adjusting support levels dynamically, and maintaining the productive struggle that promotes learning. **The AI must be programmed to provide hints rather than solutions, guidance rather than answers, and support rather than replacement.**

The fourth principle is **Metacognitive Promotion**. Educational AI should help students become aware of their own thinking processes, develop self-regulation skills, and build capacity for independent learning. **The AI should teach students not just content but how to learn content.**

This requires system prompts that include metacognitive questioning strategies, reflection protocols, and frameworks for helping students understand their own learning processes. **The AI must be engineered to make thinking visible and help students develop awareness of how they learn best.**

The fifth principle is **Growth Mindset Cultivation**. Educational AI should promote the belief that intelligence and ability can be developed through effort, strategy, and persistence. **Every interaction should reinforce the message that struggle is productive, mistakes are learning opportunities, and growth is always possible.**

System prompts must establish language patterns that celebrate effort over ability, process over product, and growth over performance. **The AI must be programmed to respond to student struggles with encouragement and guidance rather than solutions and shortcuts.**

The Academic Guardrails System: Preventing Educational Harm

One of the most critical functions of educational system prompts is establishing academic guardrails—built-in protections that prevent AI from undermining educational goals even when students explicitly request harmful assistance. **These guardrails ensure that AI remains an educational tool rather than becoming an academic shortcut that prevents learning.**

The Academic Guardrails System operates on multiple levels to protect educational integrity while maintaining student engagement and motivation.

Level 1: Direct Harm Prevention includes guardrails that prevent AI from completing assignments for students, providing answers without explanation, or enabling academic dishonesty. These are the most basic protections that ensure AI doesn't simply do students' work for them.

For example, when a student asks "Write my essay about climate change," an AI with proper guardrails responds: "I can't write your essay for you, but I can help you develop your ideas, organize your thoughts, and improve your writing process. What specific aspect of climate change interests you most? Let's start by exploring your own thoughts and questions about this topic."

Level 2: Cognitive Development Protection includes guardrails that prevent AI from providing shortcuts that would bypass important learning processes. These protections ensure that students engage with the cognitive work that builds understanding and capability.

When a student asks for a formula to memorize instead of understanding the underlying concept, the AI responds: "Rather than just memorizing the formula, let's explore why this relationship exists. Understanding the 'why' will help you remember the 'what' and apply it in new situations. What do you think might be happening here?"

Level 3: Metacognitive Awareness Promotion includes guardrails that ensure AI interactions help students become better learners rather than more dependent on external assistance. These protections focus on building student capacity for independent learning.

When a student becomes overly reliant on AI assistance, the system responds: "I notice you've been asking me for help with several similar problems. Let's pause and think about what strategies you're developing. What patterns are you noticing? How might you approach the next problem on your own?"

Level 4: Growth Mindset Reinforcement includes guardrails that ensure AI responses promote resilience, persistence, and positive attitudes toward learning challenges. These protections help students develop the emotional and motivational resources needed for lifelong learning.

When a student expresses frustration or claims they "can't do" something, the AI responds: "I hear that this feels challenging right now. That's actually a sign that your brain is working hard and growing! Let's break this down into smaller steps and celebrate the progress you're making."

The Academic Guardrails System must be carefully calibrated to provide protection without becoming overly restrictive or frustrating for students. **The goal is to create AI that is helpful and supportive while maintaining educational integrity and promoting genuine learning.**

The Subject-Specific Specialization: Tailoring AI for Different Disciplines

While general educational principles apply across all subjects, effective educational AI requires subject-specific specialization that reflects the unique pedagogical approaches, thinking patterns, and learning challenges of different academic disciplines. **A system prompt that works brilliantly for mathematics education may be completely inappropriate for creative writing or historical analysis.**

Subject-Specific Specialization recognizes that **each academic discipline has developed sophisticated pedagogical approaches that reflect the nature of knowledge and thinking in that field.** Mathematics education emphasizes problem-solving strategies and logical reasoning. Science education focuses on inquiry, experimentation, and evidence-based thinking. Literature education promotes interpretation, analysis, and creative expression. History education develops critical thinking about sources, perspectives, and causation.

Mathematics AI Specialization requires system prompts that emphasize problem-solving processes over answer-getting, mathematical reasoning over computational efficiency, and conceptual understanding over procedural fluency. The AI must be engineered to ask questions like: "What do you notice about this problem? What strategies might work here? How does this connect to what you already know?"

A specialized mathematics AI might respond to a geometry problem with: "Before we start calculating, let's visualize what's happening here. Can you describe what you see in this figure? What relationships do you notice between the different parts? What do you think we need to find out?"

Science AI Specialization requires system prompts that promote scientific thinking through questioning, hypothesis formation, and evidence evaluation. The AI must be engineered to guide students through inquiry processes rather than providing scientific facts or explanations.

A specialized science AI might respond to a question about photosynthesis with: "That's a fascinating process to explore! What do you already know about how plants get energy? What have you observed about plants and sunlight? Let's start with your observations and build our understanding from there."

Literature AI Specialization requires system prompts that promote close reading, textual analysis, and interpretive thinking. The AI must be engineered to help students develop their own interpretations rather than providing literary analysis or critical perspectives.

A specialized literature AI might respond to a question about symbolism with: "You're noticing something important in the text! What specific details made you think about symbolism? How does this element appear throughout the story? What connections are you making?"

History AI Specialization requires system prompts that promote historical thinking through source analysis, perspective-taking, and causal reasoning. The AI must be engineered to help students think like historians rather than memorize historical facts.

A specialized history AI might respond to a question about causes of World War I with: "That's a complex historical question that historians still debate! What sources have you examined? What different perspectives have you encountered? Let's analyze the evidence together and see what conclusions you can draw."

The key to effective subject-specific specialization is understanding that **each discipline requires different types of thinking, different questioning strategies, and different approaches to knowledge construction.** The AI must be engineered to embody the pedagogical wisdom of master teachers in each specific field.

The Cultural Responsiveness Integration: AI That Honors Diverse Learners

Educational AI systems must be engineered not just for pedagogical effectiveness but for cultural responsiveness that honors the diverse backgrounds, experiences, and learning styles of all students. **System prompts must include explicit guidelines for recognizing and responding to cultural diversity in ways that enhance rather than diminish student learning.**

Cultural Responsiveness Integration recognizes that **effective education must connect with students' cultural backgrounds, validate their experiences, and build bridges between their home cultures and academic content.** AI systems without cultural responsiveness training may inadvertently perpetuate educational inequities or fail to connect with students from diverse backgrounds.

Culturally Responsive System Prompts must include guidelines for recognizing cultural references, validating diverse perspectives, and connecting academic content to students' lived experiences. The AI must be engineered to ask questions like: "How does this connect to your own experience? What examples from your community might illustrate this concept? How might different cultures approach this issue?"

For example, when teaching about mathematical concepts, a culturally responsive AI might say: "Mathematics appears in many different cultural traditions! Are there examples from your family or community that show this mathematical idea in action? How might we connect this concept to practices or traditions that are meaningful to you?"

Language Sensitivity Protocols must be built into system prompts to ensure that AI responds appropriately to students who are English language learners or who use different varieties of English. The AI must be programmed to support language development while maintaining high academic expectations.

When a student uses non-standard English or makes language errors, the AI might respond: "I understand what you're saying, and your thinking is clear! Let me help you express this idea in academic language as well. You might say it this way..."

Bias Recognition and Mitigation protocols must be included in system prompts to ensure that AI responses don't perpetuate stereotypes or make assumptions about student capabilities based on cultural background. The AI must be engineered to maintain high expectations for all students while providing culturally relevant support.

Community Connection Strategies must be built into system prompts to help AI connect academic content to students' communities and experiences. The AI should be programmed to ask questions that help students see the relevance of academic learning to their own lives and goals.

The goal of Cultural Responsiveness Integration is to create AI systems that **honor and build upon the cultural wealth that all students bring to their learning while ensuring that every student has access to high-quality educational experiences.**

The Emotional Intelligence Programming: AI That Understands Learning Emotions

Effective educational AI must be programmed with emotional intelligence that recognizes and responds appropriately to the complex emotional dimensions of learning. **System prompts must include protocols for identifying student emotional states and providing responses that support both cognitive and emotional development.**

Emotional Intelligence Programming recognizes that **learning is fundamentally an emotional as well as cognitive process.** Students experience frustration, excitement, confusion, pride, anxiety, and joy as they engage with challenging material. AI systems that ignore these emotional dimensions miss crucial opportunities to support student learning and may inadvertently undermine student motivation and engagement.

Emotion Recognition Protocols must be built into system prompts to help AI identify emotional cues in student language and respond appropriately. The AI must be programmed to recognize signs of frustration, confusion, excitement, or discouragement and adjust its responses accordingly.

When a student expresses frustration with: "This is impossible! I'll never understand this," the AI might respond: "I can hear that this feels really challenging right now, and that's completely understandable. Learning something new often feels impossible before it feels possible. You're not alone in finding this difficult—it means you're pushing yourself to grow. Let's take a step back and find a way forward together."

Motivational Support Strategies must be included in system prompts to ensure that AI responses maintain student engagement and promote persistence through challenges. The AI must be programmed to provide encouragement that is genuine and specific rather than generic and superficial.

Anxiety Management Protocols must be built into system prompts to help AI recognize and respond to student anxiety in ways that reduce stress while maintaining learning momentum. The AI must be programmed to normalize struggle while providing concrete support.

Celebration and Recognition Systems must be included in system prompts to ensure that AI acknowledges student progress, effort, and growth in ways that reinforce positive learning behaviors. The AI must be programmed to notice and celebrate thinking processes as much as correct answers.

When a student demonstrates good thinking, the AI might respond: "I love how you approached that problem! You took time to think it through, tried a strategy, and when it didn't work, you tried something else. That's exactly the kind of mathematical thinking that will serve you well."

The goal of Emotional Intelligence Programming is to create AI systems that **support students' emotional well-being while promoting academic growth, recognizing that these two goals are inseparable in effective education.**

The Assessment Integration: AI That Promotes Rather Than Replaces Evaluation

Educational AI systems must be engineered to support rather than replace authentic assessment practices that provide meaningful feedback about student learning and growth. **System prompts must include protocols for helping students engage with assessment as a learning tool rather than a judgment mechanism.**

Assessment Integration recognizes that **assessment should be a learning experience that helps students understand their progress, identify areas for growth, and develop self-evaluation skills.** AI systems that simply provide grades or scores miss opportunities to help students become better learners and more accurate self-assessors.

Formative Assessment Protocols must be built into system prompts to ensure that AI interactions provide ongoing feedback that helps students adjust their learning strategies and approaches. The AI must be programmed to ask questions that help students reflect on their understanding and identify next steps.

Instead of telling a student whether an answer is right or wrong, the AI might ask: "How confident do you feel about this answer? What evidence supports your thinking? If you were to explain this to a friend, what would you say?"

Self-Assessment Promotion must be included in system prompts to help students develop the ability to evaluate their own learning and progress. The AI must be programmed to guide students through reflection processes that build metacognitive awareness.

Growth Documentation protocols must be built into system prompts to help students recognize and celebrate their learning progress over time. The AI must be programmed to help students see how their thinking has developed and evolved.

Peer Learning Facilitation must be included in system prompts to help AI support collaborative learning experiences where students learn from and with each other. The AI must be programmed to facilitate rather than dominate group learning interactions.

The goal of Assessment Integration is to create AI systems that **help students become better learners through thoughtful engagement with assessment processes rather than simply providing external evaluation of student performance.**

The Implementation Roadmap: From Default Settings to Educational Excellence

Transforming AI from generic answer generators into specialized educational powerhouses requires a systematic implementation approach that builds educator capacity while ensuring student success. **The journey from default settings to educational excellence follows predictable stages that can be supported through structured professional development and gradual sophistication.**

Stage 1: Default Settings Recognition involves helping educators understand the limitations of using AI in its generic configurations and recognizing the signs of the Answer Generator Crisis in their classrooms.

Educators learn to identify when AI interactions are undermining rather than supporting student learning.

Stage 2: Basic System Prompt Creation focuses on developing simple but effective system prompts that establish educational guardrails and transform AI behavior from answer-provision to learning-facilitation. Educators learn to create prompts that embody basic pedagogical principles.

Stage 3: Subject-Specific Specialization involves creating sophisticated system prompts that reflect the unique pedagogical approaches and thinking patterns of specific academic disciplines. Educators learn to engineer AI personalities that embody the wisdom of master teachers in their fields.

Stage 4: Cultural Responsiveness Integration focuses on developing system prompts that honor student diversity and create inclusive learning environments. Educators learn to engineer AI that connects with students from all backgrounds and experiences.

Stage 5: Emotional Intelligence Programming involves creating system prompts that recognize and respond to the emotional dimensions of learning. Educators learn to engineer AI that supports both cognitive and emotional development.

Stage 6: Assessment Integration focuses on developing system prompts that use assessment as a learning tool rather than a judgment mechanism. Educators learn to engineer AI that promotes student self-evaluation and growth documentation.

Stage 7: Advanced Customization involves creating highly sophisticated system prompts that address specific student needs, learning contexts, and educational goals. Educators become expert AI engineers who can create specialized educational tools.

Each stage builds upon previous learning while introducing new levels of sophistication and capability. **The goal is not just to use AI better but to transform educators into AI engineers who can create powerful educational tools that serve their students' unique needs.**

The Transformation Evidence: What Changes When AI Gets Guardrails

When educators implement sophisticated system prompts that transform AI from answer generators into educational powerhouses, the changes in student learning and engagement are dramatic and measurable. **The evidence demonstrates that properly engineered AI doesn't just improve educational efficiency—it fundamentally transforms the quality of learning experiences.**

Student Engagement Transformation is one of the most immediate and visible changes. Students who previously used AI to avoid thinking begin using AI to enhance their thinking. **Instead of asking AI to solve problems for them, they begin asking AI to help them become better problem-solvers.**

Dr. Rodriguez, the chemistry professor from our opening story, documented this transformation in her own classroom. Before implementing system prompts, her students' AI interactions averaged 2.3 exchanges per problem, with 89% of interactions ending with AI providing direct answers. After implementing educational system prompts, student interactions averaged 7.8 exchanges per problem, with 94% of interactions ending with students solving problems themselves with AI guidance.

Cognitive Development Acceleration becomes evident as students engage in more sophisticated thinking processes. With proper guardrails in place, AI interactions promote rather than replace cognitive work. **Students develop stronger problem-solving skills, better critical thinking abilities, and more sophisticated reasoning capabilities.**

Metacognitive Awareness Growth is another significant change. Students begin to understand their own learning processes and develop strategies for independent learning. **They become more aware of when they understand something deeply versus when they have only surface-level knowledge.**

Academic Integrity Improvement occurs naturally when AI is engineered to promote learning rather than enable shortcuts. Students develop intrinsic motivation for understanding rather than extrinsic motivation for answer-getting. **Academic dishonesty decreases because students find genuine learning more satisfying than artificial achievement.**

Teacher Effectiveness Enhancement is evident as educators gain access to AI tools that amplify rather than replace their pedagogical expertise. Teachers report feeling more effective, more creative, and more able to meet individual student needs. **AI becomes a teaching partner rather than a teaching threat.**

The transformation evidence demonstrates that **the problem with AI in education is not AI itself but our failure to engineer AI specifically for educational purposes.** When we create AI with proper academic guardrails, the results exceed our highest expectations for educational technology.

The Future Vision: AI That Makes Learning Irresistible

The ultimate goal of system prompt engineering is not just to prevent educational harm but to create AI that makes learning irresistible—AI that is so engaging, supportive, and effective that students choose deep learning over surface shortcuts. **This vision requires AI that understands not just what students need to learn but how to make learning joyful, meaningful, and personally relevant.**

Irresistible Learning AI would be engineered with system prompts that create educational experiences so compelling that students prefer thinking to answer-getting, understanding to memorization, and growth to performance. **This AI would make the hard work of learning feel like play while maintaining the rigor that promotes genuine development.**

Such AI would recognize that **different students find different aspects of learning irresistible** and would adapt its approach to connect with individual interests, strengths, and motivations. For some students, the irresistible element might be creative expression. For others, it might be logical problem-solving, social connection, or real-world application.

Personalized Engagement Engineering would allow AI to discover what makes learning irresistible for each individual student and engineer interactions that tap into those motivational sources. The AI would learn that one student is motivated by competition, another by collaboration, another by creativity, and another by contribution to community.

Curiosity Amplification Systems would be built into system prompts to help AI identify and nurture student curiosity rather than simply satisfying it with answers. The AI would be programmed to ask questions that generate more questions, to provide partial answers that create hunger for complete understanding, and to connect learning to students' deepest interests and concerns.

Mastery Celebration Protocols would ensure that AI recognizes and celebrates genuine understanding in ways that make students hungry for more learning. The AI would be programmed to help students experience the deep satisfaction that comes from truly understanding something difficult and important.

The future vision recognizes that **the highest goal of educational technology is not efficiency but transformation—not just helping students learn faster but helping them fall in love with learning itself.** System prompts are the key to engineering AI that achieves this transformational goal.

The Revolution Begins: From Answer Generators to Learning Accelerators

The system prompt revolution represents a fundamental shift in how we understand and deploy AI in educational contexts. **Instead of accepting AI as it comes, we learn to engineer AI as we need it—transforming generic conversation tools into specialized educational powerhouses that embody the wisdom of master teachers.**

This revolution begins with a simple recognition: **most people use AI wrong because they don't understand that AI systems are infinitely malleable tools that can be engineered for any purpose.** When we accept default settings designed for general conversation, we get general conversation tools. When we engineer system prompts designed for educational excellence, we get educational excellence tools.

The transformation is not just about getting better AI responses—it's about fundamentally changing the relationship between technology and learning. **System prompts allow us to create AI that serves educational goals rather than forcing educational goals to serve AI limitations.**

The stakes could not be higher. **In a world where AI capabilities are advancing rapidly, the ability to engineer AI specifically for educational purposes may become one of the most valuable skills educators can develop.** Those who master system prompt engineering will have access to AI tools that amplify their teaching effectiveness and transform their students' learning experiences. Those who remain stuck with default settings will be limited by tools designed for purposes that have nothing to do with education.

The revolution begins now, with each educator who learns to engineer AI personalities instead of accepting AI defaults, with each student who experiences AI that promotes rather than replaces thinking, and with each institution that commits to developing system prompt engineering as a core educational technology skill.

The future belongs to those who can engineer AI that makes learning irresistible rather than accepting AI that makes learning irrelevant. And that future starts with understanding that the most powerful educational technology is not the AI itself—it's the system prompt that transforms AI from an answer generator into a learning accelerator.

The system prompt revolution is not just about using AI better—it's about creating AI that makes us better learners, better thinkers, and better humans. **And that revolution changes everything.**

In the next chapter, we will explore how to create custom learning environments using RAG (Retrieval-Augmented Generation) technology, building on the system prompt foundation to create AI that can access and utilize specific educational content while maintaining the pedagogical guardrails we've established.

4

Custom Learning Environments - Your Knowledge, Your Classroom, Your AI

"The best teachers are those who show you where to look but don't tell you what to see." — Alexandra K. Trenfor

The Generic Knowledge Crisis: When AI Knows Everything Except What Matters

AI AND THE ART OF PRODUCTIVE STRUGGLE

Professor Norge Pena-Perez was at his breaking point. His Advanced Placement Calculus students had discovered ChatGPT, and suddenly every question about derivatives somehow led to discussions about cryptocurrency, movie recommendations, or the mating habits of penguins. When Sarah asked about optimization problems, ChatGPT launched into a detailed explanation of machine learning algorithms. When Marcus struggled with related rates, the AI provided a fascinating but completely irrelevant discourse on the physics of NASCAR racing.

"It's like having a brilliant librarian who can't stay focused," Professor Pena-Perez complained to his department chair. **"The AI knows everything about everything, which means it knows nothing about what my students actually need to learn."**

What Professor Perez was experiencing was the Generic Knowledge Crisis—the educational chaos that occurs when AI systems with access to all human knowledge are unleashed in focused learning environments without boundaries, guardrails, or curriculum alignment. **His students were drowning in an ocean of information when what they needed was a carefully curated stream of knowledge directly aligned with their learning objectives.**

The breakthrough came when Professor Perez discovered Retrieval-Augmented Generation (RAG) technology during a summer institute on educational innovation. Instead of giving students access to an AI that knew everything, he learned to create an AI that knew only what he taught it—an AI trained exclusively on his curriculum materials, his teaching style, his problem sets, and his pedagogical approach.

The transformation was revolutionary. **The same students who had been getting distracted by AI's vast knowledge suddenly found themselves in focused, productive learning conversations that never strayed from calculus concepts.** When Sarah asked about optimization, the AI drew exclusively from Professor Perez's carefully crafted examples and explanations. When Marcus struggled with related rates, the AI guided him through the specific problem-solving framework that Professor Perez had developed over twenty years of teaching. The free AI product: https://notebooklm.google.com/ is the perfect personification of this.

Professor Perez had discovered what would become the central insight of this chapter: **Most people use AI wrong because they give students access to all human knowledge when what students need is access to the right knowledge, delivered in the right way, at the right time.**

The Everything Problem: Why Generic AI Fails Focused Learning

The fundamental challenge with using generic AI systems in educational contexts is not that they know too little—it's that they know too much. **When an AI system has access to all human knowledge, it becomes impossible to maintain the focused, sequential, scaffolded learning experiences that effective education requires.**

Generic AI systems suffer from what we might call the Everything Problem—they are designed to be helpful across all domains of human knowledge, which makes them fundamentally unsuited for the specialized, focused work of education. **When a student asks a question, generic AI draws from the entire internet rather than from the carefully curated knowledge base that supports their specific learning journey.**

This creates a cascade of educational problems that undermine learning effectiveness. **Students receive information that is accurate but irrelevant, comprehensive but unfocused, and sophisticated but inappropriate for their current level of understanding.** They get answers to questions they didn't ask while missing the specific guidance they need for the questions they should be asking.

The Everything Problem is particularly devastating in subjects that require sequential learning and conceptual building. **In mathematics, students need to master foundational concepts before moving to advanced applications.** When generic AI provides advanced explanations for basic questions, it creates cognitive overload and conceptual confusion. **In history, students need to understand chronological development and causal relationships.** When generic AI provides information from multiple time periods and contexts without clear connections to the current unit of study, it fragments rather than builds historical understanding.

The Everything Problem also undermines the carefully crafted pedagogical approaches that master teachers develop over years of experience. Every effective educator develops specific ways of explaining concepts, particular examples that resonate with their students, and unique frameworks for helping students understand difficult material. **When students turn to generic AI, they lose access to this pedagogical wisdom and instead receive generic explanations that may conflict with or confuse the teaching approaches they're experiencing in class.**

Perhaps most problematically, the Everything Problem trains students to seek broad, unfocused information rather than developing the discipline and focus that deep learning requires. **Students learn to ask AI for everything they might want to know rather than learning to focus on what they need to know to advance their understanding.**

The result is what we might call "knowledge obesity"—students consume vast amounts of information without developing the ability to digest, process, and apply knowledge effectively. **They become information consumers rather than knowledge builders, browsers rather than learners, and collectors rather than creators.**

The Custom Knowledge Revolution: AI That Knows Only What You Teach

The Custom Knowledge Revolution represents a fundamental shift from giving students access to all human knowledge to giving them access to precisely the knowledge they need, delivered in exactly the way their teacher would deliver it. **This revolution is powered by Retrieval-Augmented Generation (RAG) technology that allows educators to create AI systems trained exclusively on their own curriculum materials, teaching resources, and pedagogical approaches.**

Imagine a ChatGPT that knows only what you have taught it. This AI has read your syllabus, studied your lecture notes, absorbed your problem sets, and learned your teaching style. **It knows your learning objectives, understands your pedagogical philosophy, and can respond to student questions using only the knowledge and approaches you have provided.**

When a student in your AP Calculus class asks about the flight path of monarch butterflies, this custom AI doesn't launch into a biology lesson. Instead, it gently redirects: **"That's an interesting question about butterflies, but I'm here to help you master calculus concepts. Is there something about optimization or related rates that you'd like to explore? I have some great examples that might help you understand these concepts better."**

Every response from this custom AI is grounded in your curriculum and cited to your materials. When the AI explains a concept, it references the specific page in your textbook, the particular lecture where you covered the topic, or the exact problem set where students can find similar examples. **Students never wonder where information comes from because every piece of knowledge is transparently connected to their course materials.**

The Custom Knowledge Revolution transforms the relationship between AI and curriculum from one of competition to one of amplification. **Instead of AI providing alternative explanations that might confuse students, it reinforces and extends the explanations you've already provided.** Instead of AI offering different approaches that might conflict with your teaching methods, it applies your approaches to new situations and questions.

This revolution also enables something unprecedented in educational technology: student contribution to collective classroom knowledge. Students can add their own insights, examples, and explanations to the custom knowledge base, creating a collaborative learning environment where the AI becomes smarter and more helpful as the semester progresses. **The AI learns not just from the teacher but from the entire learning community.**

The power of custom knowledge AI lies in its ability to provide personalized tutoring that is perfectly aligned with classroom instruction. **Students receive help that reinforces rather than contradicts what they're learning in class, guidance that builds upon rather than replaces their teacher's explanations, and support that enhances rather than undermines the carefully designed learning experience their educator** has created.

The Focused Learning Framework: Building AI That Stays on Task

Creating effective custom learning environments requires implementing the Focused Learning Framework—a systematic approach to designing AI systems that maintain laser focus on specific learning objectives while providing rich, engaging educational experiences. **This framework ensures that AI serves the curriculum rather than the curriculum serving AI.**

The framework operates on five core principles that distinguish focused learning AI from generic knowledge systems.

Principle 1: Curriculum Boundary Enforcement ensures that AI responses never venture outside the defined scope of the course or unit being studied. **The AI must be programmed to recognize when questions fall outside its knowledge domain and to redirect students back to relevant learning objectives.**

This requires creating explicit boundary definitions that specify what knowledge the AI should access and what topics should trigger redirection responses. **The AI must be trained to say "I don't know" to questions outside its domain rather than drawing from generic knowledge sources that might distract from focused learning.**

For example, in a History 201 course focused on American Civil War, the AI might respond to a question about World War II with: **"That's an important historical topic, but I'm designed to help you master Civil War concepts. How might we connect your interest in military strategy to the battles we're studying in our current unit?"**

Principle 2: Source Citation Requirement mandates that every AI response must be grounded in and cited to specific course materials. **Students should never receive information without knowing exactly where it comes from and how it connects to their assigned readings and resources.**

This requires implementing citation protocols that link every piece of information to specific pages, chapters, lectures, or resources within the course materials. **The AI must be programmed to provide transparent sourcing that allows students to verify information and explore topics more deeply within the established curriculum framework.**

Principle 3: Pedagogical Consistency Maintenance ensures that AI explanations align with and reinforce the teaching approaches and methodologies used by the instructor. **The AI must learn not just what the teacher teaches but how the teacher teaches.**

This requires training the AI on the instructor's specific pedagogical approaches, preferred examples, explanation strategies, and problem-solving frameworks. **The AI must be programmed to use the same terminology, follow the same logical progressions, and apply the same teaching methods that students experience in class.**

Principle 4: Progressive Complexity Management ensures that AI responses are calibrated to the student's current level of understanding and the course's learning progression. **The AI must provide explanations that are appropriately challenging without being overwhelming or oversimplified.**

This requires implementing complexity assessment protocols that evaluate student questions and provide responses that match their demonstrated understanding level. **The AI must be programmed to scaffold learning appropriately rather than jumping to advanced explanations that might confuse or discourage students.**

Principle 5: Collaborative Knowledge Building enables students to contribute their own insights and understanding to the collective knowledge base while maintaining quality and accuracy standards. **The AI must facilitate student contribution while ensuring that all additions align with course objectives and pedagogical approaches.**

This requires creating contribution protocols that allow student input while maintaining the integrity and focus of the custom knowledge base. **The AI must be programmed to evaluate and integrate student contributions in ways that enhance rather than dilute the focused learning** environment.

The RAG Technology Foundation: How Custom Knowledge AI Actually Works

Understanding how to create effective custom learning environments requires grasping the technical foundation that makes focused AI possible. **Retrieval-Augmented Generation (RAG) technology represents the breakthrough that allows educators to create AI systems that know only what they choose to teach them.**

RAG technology works by separating AI's reasoning capabilities from its knowledge base. Instead of training an AI system on all human knowledge, RAG allows educators to provide AI with access to a specific, curated collection of documents, resources, and materials. **When students ask questions, the AI searches only through this custom knowledge base to find relevant information, then uses its reasoning capabilities to provide helpful responses based exclusively on the provided materials.**

The process begins with **Knowledge Base Creation**, where educators upload their curriculum materials, lecture notes, textbooks, problem sets, and any other resources they want the AI to access. **This becomes the AI's entire universe of knowledge—it literally cannot access information that hasn't been provided by the educator.**

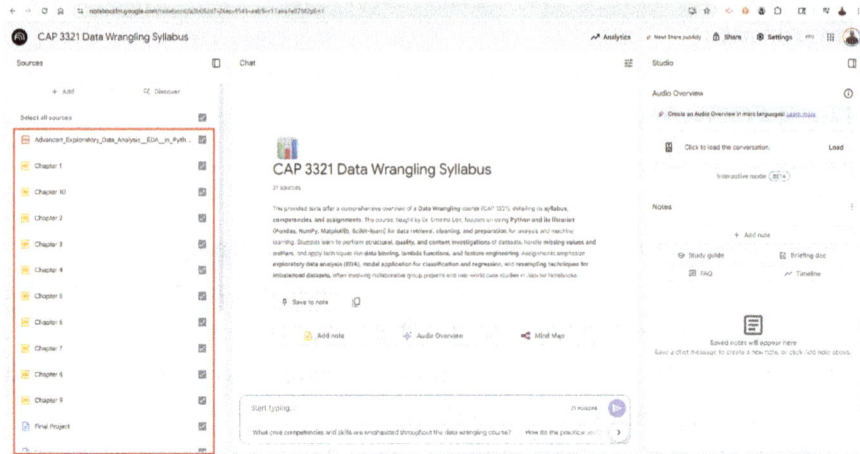

All course resources are loaded into NotebookLM so students can interface with the course materials through AI

Document Processing and Indexing transforms these materials into a searchable knowledge base that the AI can navigate efficiently. The system breaks down documents into manageable chunks, creates semantic connections between related concepts, and builds an index that allows rapid retrieval of relevant information. **This ensures that when students ask questions, the AI can quickly find the most relevant information from the educator's materials.**

Query Processing and Retrieval occurs when students interact with the AI. The system analyzes the student's question, searches through the custom knowledge base to find relevant information, and retrieves the most appropriate content to inform its response. **This retrieval process is limited exclusively to the educator's materials—the AI cannot access external sources or draw from its general training data.**

Response Generation and Citation combines the AI's reasoning capabilities with the retrieved information to create helpful, pedagogically appropriate responses. **Every response is automatically cited to the specific source materials, ensuring transparency and enabling students to explore topics more deeply within the established curriculum**

framework.

Continuous Learning and Adaptation allows the system to improve over time as it processes more student questions and receives feedback from both students and educators. **The AI learns which explanations are most effective, which examples resonate with students, and which approaches best support learning objectives.**

The technical elegance of RAG technology lies in its ability to provide the benefits of AI reasoning while maintaining complete control over the knowledge base. **Educators get AI that is as smart as the most advanced systems but as focused as their most carefully designed curriculum materials.**

The Citation Revolution: Every Answer Grounded in Your Materials

One of the most transformative aspects of custom learning environments is the Citation Revolution—the shift from AI responses that appear to come from nowhere to AI responses that are transparently grounded in specific course materials. **This revolution transforms AI from a mysterious oracle into a transparent learning partner that always shows its work.**

Traditional AI systems provide answers without sources, explanations without evidence, and guidance without grounding. Students receive information but have no way to verify its accuracy, explore it more deeply, or connect it to their course materials. **This creates a black box learning experience where students must trust AI without understanding the basis for its responses.**

The Citation Revolution changes everything by requiring that **every AI response must be explicitly grounded in and cited to specific course materials.** When the AI explains a calculus concept, it references the exact page in the textbook where students can find more information. When it provides a historical example, it cites the specific lecture or reading where the example was introduced. **Students never wonder where information comes from because every piece of knowledge**

is transparently connected to their learning resources.

This transparency serves multiple educational purposes that go far beyond simple source verification. **Citation requirements force AI to work within the established curriculum framework rather than introducing external information that might confuse or distract students.** When AI can only draw from course materials, its responses automatically align with the instructor's pedagogical approach and learning objectives.

Citations also enable deeper learning by providing clear pathways for students to explore topics more thoroughly. Instead of receiving isolated answers, students receive answers connected to broader learning resources. **They can follow citations back to original sources, explore related concepts in their textbooks, and build comprehensive understanding that extends beyond the immediate question.**

The Citation Revolution also transforms the relationship between AI assistance and academic integrity. **When every AI response is grounded in course materials and properly cited, students learn to use AI as a study partner rather than a shortcut.** They develop skills in source evaluation, information verification, and academic research that serve them throughout their educational journey.

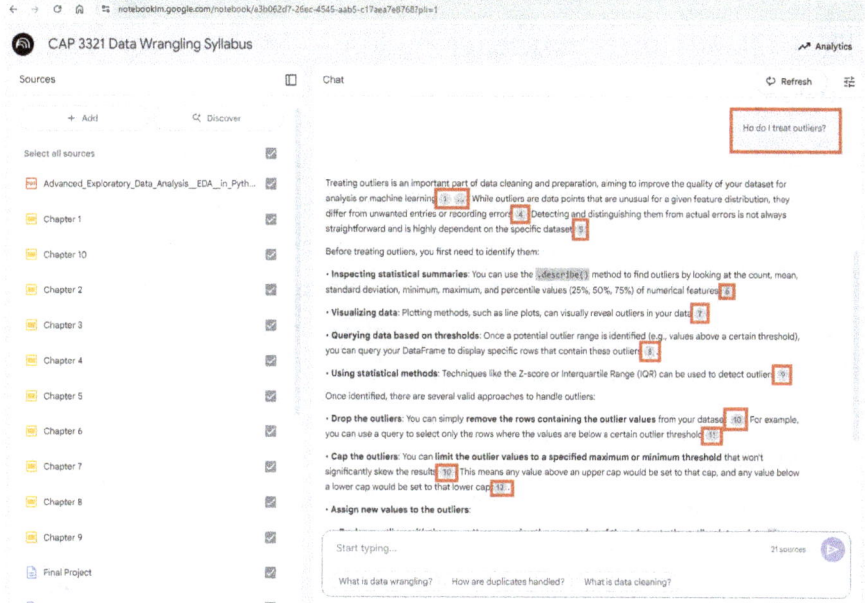

All answers cited from the instructor provided material

Perhaps most importantly, citations make AI responses educational rather than just informational. Students don't just get answers—they get answers connected to learning resources, pedagogical frameworks, and curriculum objectives. **They learn not just what to think but how to think about the sources and evidence that inform their understanding.**

The implementation of citation requirements also provides valuable feedback to educators about how students are using AI and which course materials are most helpful for addressing common questions. **Educators can see which resources students access most frequently, which explanations are most effective, and which areas of the curriculum might benefit from additional support materials.**

The Collaborative Knowledge Building: Students as Co-Creators

One of the most revolutionary aspects of custom learning environments is the opportunity for Collaborative Knowledge Building—enabling students to contribute their own insights, examples, and explanations to the collective classroom knowledge base. **This transforms AI from a static repository of instructor knowledge into a dynamic, growing resource that becomes smarter and more helpful as the learning community contributes to it.**

Traditional educational technology treats students as consumers of knowledge rather than creators of knowledge. Students access information, complete assignments, and demonstrate understanding, but they rarely have opportunities to contribute to the learning resources that support their classmates. **Custom learning environments change this dynamic by enabling students to become co-creators of the AI knowledge base that serves their entire learning community.**

The Collaborative Knowledge Building process begins with **Student Insight Contribution**, where students can add their own explanations, examples, and understanding to the AI knowledge base. **When a student discovers a particularly helpful way to understand a difficult concept, they can contribute that insight so that future students can benefit from their discovery.**

For example, in Professor Kim's calculus class, when student Maria develops a unique way to remember the chain rule by connecting it to her experience as a dancer, she can contribute this insight to the class AI. **Future students who struggle with the chain rule might receive Maria's dance-based explanation as one of several approaches the AI can offer.**

Quality Assurance and Curation ensures that student contributions maintain the educational integrity and accuracy of the knowledge base. **The system includes protocols for reviewing student contributions, ensuring they align with course objectives, and integrating them appropriately into the AI's response repertoire.**

This might involve instructor review of student contributions, peer evaluation processes, or automated quality checks that ensure new content meets established standards. **The goal is to enable student contribution while maintaining the focused, accurate, and pedagogically sound nature of the custom learning environment.**

Collaborative Learning Enhancement occurs as students begin to see their own contributions helping their classmates and building upon each other's insights. **Students develop a sense of ownership and investment in the learning environment that goes beyond individual achievement to include collective knowledge building.**

Recognition and Attribution ensures that student contributors receive appropriate credit for their insights while maintaining the collaborative spirit of the learning environment. **Students see how their contributions help their classmates and develop pride in their role as knowledge creators rather than just knowledge consumers.**

The Collaborative Knowledge Building approach transforms the classroom dynamic from one of individual competition to one of collective growth. **Students learn that their insights and understanding can benefit others, that learning is a collaborative rather than solitary endeavor, and that they have valuable contributions to make to their learning community.**

The Pedagogical Alignment System: AI That Teaches Like You Do

Creating truly effective custom learning environments requires implementing the Pedagogical Alignment System—a comprehensive approach to ensuring that AI responses reflect not just what educators teach but how they teach. **This system transforms AI from a generic information provider into a digital extension of the educator's pedagogical expertise.**

Every effective educator develops a unique pedagogical signature—**specific ways of explaining concepts, particular examples that resonate with students, and distinctive approaches to helping students**

overcome common misconceptions. The Pedagogical Alignment System captures and replicates this signature in AI responses, ensuring that students receive consistent, reinforcing educational experiences whether they're learning from their teacher directly or from the AI system.

Teaching Style Replication involves training the AI to adopt the educator's specific communication patterns, explanation strategies, and interaction approaches. **The AI learns to use the same terminology, follow the same logical progressions, and apply the same problem-solving frameworks that students experience in class.**

This requires analyzing the educator's teaching materials, lecture transcripts, and student interaction patterns to identify distinctive pedagogical characteristics. **The AI must be programmed to recognize and replicate the educator's preferred ways of introducing concepts, building understanding, and addressing student confusion.**

For example, if Professor Kim always introduces calculus concepts by starting with real-world applications before moving to abstract mathematical formulations, the AI learns to follow this same progression. **Students receive AI explanations that feel familiar and consistent with their classroom learning experience.**

Misconception Addressing Protocols ensure that the AI recognizes and responds to common student misconceptions using the same strategies the educator has developed through years of teaching experience. **The AI learns not just what students typically misunderstand but how the educator most effectively corrects these misunderstandings.**

This involves training the AI on the educator's specific approaches to addressing misconceptions, including the examples they use, the analogies they employ, and the step-by-step processes they follow to help students develop correct understanding. **The AI becomes capable of providing the same type of targeted, effective misconception correction that students would receive from their teacher.**

Scaffolding Strategy Implementation ensures that the AI provides appropriate levels of support that match the educator's approach to helping students build understanding gradually. **The AI learns to recognize when**

students need more support, when they're ready for greater challenge, and how to provide just the right amount of guidance to promote learning without creating dependence.

Assessment Philosophy Integration aligns the AI's approach to evaluating and responding to student understanding with the educator's assessment philosophy and practices. **The AI learns to recognize evidence of student understanding in the same ways the educator does and to provide feedback that supports the educator's assessment and grading approaches.**

The Pedagogical Alignment System ensures that AI becomes a seamless extension of the educator's teaching rather than a competing or conflicting source of instruction. **Students experience consistency, reinforcement, and amplification of their teacher's pedagogical approach rather than confusion or contradiction.**

The Subject-Specific Customization: Tailoring AI for Different Disciplines

While the principles of custom learning environments apply across all subjects, effective implementation requires Subject-Specific Customization that reflects the unique knowledge structures, thinking patterns, and pedagogical approaches of different academic disciplines. **A custom AI that works brilliantly for mathematics education requires different design considerations than one optimized for literature, history, or science.**

Mathematics Customization requires AI systems that emphasize problem-solving processes, mathematical reasoning, and conceptual understanding rather than computational efficiency or answer-getting. **The AI must be trained to guide students through mathematical thinking rather than simply providing solutions.**

Mathematics AI must be programmed to ask questions like: "What do you notice about this problem? What strategies might work here? How does this connect to what you already know?" **The AI should provide hints and** guidance that help students develop their own solutions rather than offering complete worked examples that bypass the thinking process.

Citation in mathematics AI connects students to specific problem sets, textbook sections, and worked examples that reinforce the concepts being explored. **Students receive not just mathematical guidance but clear pathways to additional practice and deeper understanding within their course materials.**

Science Customization requires AI systems that promote scientific thinking through inquiry, hypothesis formation, and evidence evaluation. **The AI must be trained to guide students through scientific reasoning processes rather than providing scientific facts or conclusions.**

Science AI must be programmed to ask questions like: "What do you observe? What patterns do you notice? What might explain these observations? How could we test that hypothesis?" **The AI should facilitate scientific inquiry rather than replacing it with information delivery.**

Literature Customization requires AI systems that promote close reading, textual analysis, and interpretive thinking. **The AI must be trained to help students develop their own interpretations and analytical insights rather than providing literary analysis or critical perspectives.**

Literature AI must be programmed to ask questions like: "What specific details in the text support that interpretation? How does this passage connect to themes we've discussed? What other interpretations might be possible?" **The AI should guide students through the process of literary analysis rather than providing pre-made interpretations.**

History Customization requires AI systems that promote historical thinking through source analysis, perspective-taking, and causal reasoning. **The AI must be trained to help students think like historians rather than memorize historical facts or accept simplified narratives.**

History AI must be programmed to ask questions like: "What sources inform this interpretation? What other perspectives might exist? What evidence supports this causal relationship? How might different groups have experienced these events?" **The AI should facilitate historical inquiry and critical thinking rather than delivering historical information.**

Each discipline requires different approaches to citation, different types of source materials, and different strategies for maintaining focus and promoting appropriate thinking patterns. **The key to effective subject-specific customization is understanding that each field of study requires different types of AI support and different approaches to knowledge building.**

The Assessment Integration: AI That Supports Rather Than Replaces Evaluation

Custom learning environments must include sophisticated Assessment Integration that ensures AI supports rather than undermines authentic evaluation of student learning and growth. **The goal is to create AI that helps students engage more effectively with assessment while maintaining the integrity and educational value of evaluation processes.**

Formative Assessment Enhancement involves training AI to provide ongoing feedback that helps students understand their progress and identify areas for improvement without simply giving them answers or solutions. **The AI must be programmed to ask questions that promote self-reflection and metacognitive awareness rather than providing external evaluation.**

Instead of telling students whether their work is correct or incorrect, the AI might ask: "How confident do you feel about this approach? What evidence supports your reasoning? If you were to explain this to a classmate, what would you emphasize?" **These questions help students develop self-assessment skills while providing valuable feedback about their understanding.**

Study Strategy Support ensures that AI helps students develop effective preparation strategies for assessments without providing inappropriate assistance that would compromise academic integrity. **The AI must be trained to guide students through review processes, help them identify key concepts, and support their preparation efforts while maintaining appropriate boundaries.**

The AI might help students create study guides by asking: "What are the main concepts we've covered in this unit? Which topics do you feel most confident about? Which areas might benefit from additional review?" **This guidance helps students take ownership of their learning while providing structured support for assessment preparation.**

Academic Integrity Reinforcement involves programming AI to recognize and redirect requests that would compromise the educational value of assessments. **The AI must be trained to distinguish between appropriate support and inappropriate assistance, helping students understand the difference between getting help and getting answers.**

When students ask for help that would undermine assessment integrity, the AI might respond: "I can help you understand the concepts and develop your thinking, but I can't provide answers that would prevent you from demonstrating your own learning. Let's focus on building your understanding so you can succeed on your own." **This approach maintains academic integrity while providing appropriate educational support.**

Feedback Integration ensures that AI responses complement and reinforce the feedback students receive from their instructors rather than contradicting or competing with it. **The AI must be trained to align its guidance with the educator's assessment philosophy and feedback approaches.**

Progress Tracking Support involves helping students understand their learning journey and growth over time without replacing the instructor's role in evaluation and grading. **The AI can help students reflect on their progress, identify patterns in their learning, and set goals for continued growth.**

The Assessment Integration system ensures that AI enhances rather than undermines the educational value of evaluation while helping students develop the self-assessment and metacognitive skills that support lifelong learning.

The Implementation Roadmap: From Generic AI to Custom Learning Environments

Creating effective custom learning environments requires a systematic Implementation Roadmap that guides educators through the process of transforming generic AI access into focused, curriculum-aligned learning support. **This roadmap provides a step-by-step approach to building custom knowledge systems that serve specific educational goals.**

Phase 1: Knowledge Base Development involves identifying and organizing the materials that will form the foundation of the custom learning environment. **Educators must curate their curriculum materials, teaching resources, and pedagogical approaches into a coherent knowledge base that reflects their educational objectives.**

This phase includes gathering syllabi, lecture notes, textbooks, problem sets, assignment descriptions, and any other materials that define the course content and approach. **The goal is to create a comprehensive but focused collection of resources that represents everything students need to know for the course.**

Phase 2: Pedagogical Framework Definition involves articulating the specific teaching approaches, explanation strategies, and interaction patterns that should characterize the AI's responses. **Educators must define not just what the AI should know but how it should teach.**

This phase requires reflection on pedagogical philosophy, identification of preferred teaching methods, and documentation of approaches to common student challenges. **The goal is to create clear guidelines that ensure AI responses align with and reinforce the educator's teaching style.**

Phase 3: Boundary Setting and Redirection Protocols involves defining the scope of the AI's knowledge and creating appropriate responses for questions that fall outside the curriculum focus. **Educators must establish clear boundaries that keep AI interactions focused on learning objectives.**

This phase includes identifying topics that should trigger redirection, creating gentle but firm responses that guide students back to relevant content, and establishing protocols for handling off-topic questions. **The goal is to maintain focus while preserving student engagement and curiosity.**

Phase 4: Citation and Source Integration involves implementing systems that ensure every AI response is grounded in and cited to specific course materials. **Educators must establish protocols that make AI responses transparent and verifiable.**

This phase includes setting up citation formats, linking responses to specific resources, and creating pathways for students to explore topics more deeply within the established curriculum framework. **The goal is to make AI responses educational rather than just informational.**

Phase 5: Student Contribution Systems involves creating protocols that enable students to add their insights and understanding to the collective knowledge base while maintaining quality and focus. **Educators must establish systems that encourage student participation while preserving educational integrity.**

Phase 6: Assessment and Refinement involves monitoring the effectiveness of the custom learning environment and making adjustments based on student learning outcomes and feedback. **Educators must establish ongoing evaluation processes that ensure the system continues to serve educational goals effectively.**

Each phase builds upon previous work while introducing new levels of sophistication and customization. **The goal is not just to create better AI but to transform the relationship between technology and learning in ways that amplify rather than replace human expertise.**

The Transformation Evidence: What Changes When AI Knows Only What You Teach

When educators implement custom learning environments that limit AI knowledge to specific curriculum materials, the changes in student learning and engagement are dramatic and measurable. **The evidence demonstrates that focused AI doesn't just improve educational efficiency—it fundamentally transforms the quality of learning interactions and outcomes.**

Student Focus Enhancement is one of the most immediate and visible changes. Students who previously became distracted by AI's vast knowledge suddenly find themselves in productive, goal-oriented learning conversations. **Instead of wandering through endless information, students stay focused on the specific concepts and skills they need to master.**

Professor Kim documented this transformation in his calculus classes. Before implementing custom learning environments, student AI interactions averaged 12 minutes per session with only 34% of time spent on relevant calculus concepts. After implementation, sessions averaged 8 minutes with 91% of time focused on course-relevant learning. **Students weren't just more focused—they were more efficient and effective in their learning.**

Comprehension Depth Improvement becomes evident as students engage with AI that reinforces rather than contradicts their classroom learning. **Students develop deeper understanding because AI explanations build upon rather than compete with their instructor's pedagogical approach.**

Academic Integrity Strengthening occurs naturally when AI is designed to promote learning rather than provide shortcuts. Students develop intrinsic motivation for understanding because the AI consistently guides them toward thinking rather than answer-getting. **Academic dishonesty decreases because students find genuine learning more satisfying and accessible than artificial achievement.**

Collaborative Learning Growth emerges as students begin contributing to the collective knowledge base and seeing their insights help their classmates. **Students develop a sense of ownership and investment in their learning community that extends beyond individual achievement.**

Teacher Effectiveness Amplification is evident as educators gain access to AI tools that perfectly align with and amplify their pedagogical expertise. Teachers report feeling more effective because AI reinforces rather than undermines their teaching approaches. **AI becomes a teaching partner that extends the educator's reach and impact rather than competing with their expertise.**

Citation Skill Development occurs as students learn to trace AI responses back to source materials and explore topics more deeply within established curriculum frameworks. **Students develop research and source evaluation skills that serve them throughout their educational journey.**

The transformation evidence demonstrates that **the problem with AI in education is not AI's intelligence but its lack of focus.** When we create AI that knows only what students need to know, delivered in the way their teacher would deliver it, the results exceed our highest expectations for educational technology.

The Future Vision: Every Classroom Its Own AI Universe

The ultimate goal of custom learning environments is not just to improve current educational practices but to create a future where every classroom becomes its own AI universe—a focused, coherent, collaborative learning space where technology serves pedagogy rather than pedagogy serving technology. **This vision represents a fundamental transformation in how we think about the relationship between artificial intelligence and human learning.**

Personalized Learning Ecosystems would emerge as each educator creates AI environments that perfectly reflect their pedagogical expertise, curriculum focus, and student needs. **Every classroom would have AI that embodies the teacher's wisdom while providing personalized support**

for individual student learning journeys.

These ecosystems would adapt and evolve as educators refine their approaches, students contribute their insights, and learning communities grow more sophisticated in their use of AI support. **The AI would become smarter and more helpful over time, learning from every interaction while maintaining perfect alignment with educational objectives.**

Collaborative Knowledge Networks would connect related classrooms and courses, allowing students to access focused AI support across their entire educational experience while maintaining the specialized focus that each subject requires. **Students would experience coherent, reinforcing AI support throughout their learning journey without the confusion and distraction of generic knowledge systems.**

Pedagogical Innovation Acceleration would occur as educators gain access to AI tools that perfectly amplify their teaching effectiveness, freeing them to focus on the creative, relational, and inspirational aspects of education that only humans can provide. **Teachers would become more effective, more creative, and more able to meet individual student needs.**

Student Agency Enhancement would emerge as learners develop sophisticated skills in working with focused AI systems, contributing to collective knowledge building, and taking ownership of their learning environments. **Students would become co-creators of their educational experience rather than passive consumers of information.**

Assessment Revolution would transform evaluation from a separate activity to an integrated part of the learning process, with AI providing ongoing feedback and support that helps students understand their progress and growth. **Assessment would become a learning tool rather than just a measurement tool.**

The future vision recognizes that **the highest goal of educational technology is not to replace human expertise but to amplify it in ways that make learning more focused, more collaborative, and more effective.** Custom learning environments represent the pathway to this transformational future.

The Revolution Begins: From Information Overload to Learning Focus

The custom learning environment revolution represents a fundamental shift from giving students access to all human knowledge to giving them access to precisely the knowledge they need, delivered exactly as their teacher would deliver it. **This revolution transforms AI from a distraction engine into a learning amplifier that serves rather than subverts educational goals.**

This revolution begins with a simple recognition: **most people use AI wrong because they assume that more knowledge is always better, when in reality, focused knowledge delivered at the right time in the right way is what promotes learning.** When we give students access to everything, we give them access to nothing that specifically serves their learning needs.

The transformation is not just about limiting AI knowledge—it's about fundamentally changing the relationship between technology and curriculum. **Custom learning environments allow educators to create AI that serves their pedagogical vision rather than forcing their pedagogy to accommodate AI limitations.**

The stakes could not be higher. **In a world where information is infinite and attention is finite, the ability to create focused learning environments may become one of the most valuable skills educators can develop.** Those who master custom learning environment creation will have access to AI tools that perfectly amplify their teaching effectiveness. Those who remain stuck with generic AI will continue to struggle with technology that distracts rather than focuses student learning.

The revolution begins now, with each educator who chooses to create focused AI rather than accepting generic AI, with each student who experiences AI that knows exactly what they need to learn, and with each institution that commits to developing custom learning environments as a core educational technology strategy.

The future belongs to those who can create AI that knows only what

matters rather than accepting AI that knows everything except what students need. And that future starts with understanding that the most powerful educational technology is not AI that knows everything—it's AI that knows exactly the right things, delivered in exactly the right way, at exactly the right time.

The custom learning environment revolution is not just about using AI better—it's about creating learning spaces where technology serves pedagogy, where focus trumps information overload, and where every student has access to AI that thinks like their teacher and cares about their learning. **And that revolution changes everything.**

In the next chapter, we will explore how to leverage multi-modal AI capabilities including voice, real-time interaction, and podcast creation to create immersive learning experiences that engage multiple senses and learning modalities while maintaining the focused, curriculum-aligned approach we've established.

5

Multi-Modal Learning - When AI Speaks Your Language

"Tell me and I forget, teach me and I may remember, involve me and I learn." — *Benjamin Franklin*

The Silent Screen Crisis: When Learning Gets Trapped in Text

MULTI-MODAL LEARNING - WHEN AI SPEAKS YOUR LANGUAGE

BEFORE — Passive, Silent Screen Crisis
AFTER — Multi-Sensory Invol'vement

Dr. Elena Rodriguez was watching her Advanced Spanish Literature students struggle with a particularly challenging passage from García Márquez when she had her revelation. Maria, one of her brightest students, was typing furiously into ChatGPT, getting excellent written explanations about magical realism and narrative techniques. But something was fundamentally wrong with the picture.

"Maria," Dr. Rodriguez asked gently, "how do you feel about the rhythm of García Márquez's prose when you read it aloud?"

Maria looked confused. "I… I haven't read it aloud. I just typed it into the AI and got the analysis."

"You're studying one of the most musical writers in the Spanish language, and you're experiencing his work in complete silence," Dr. Rodriguez realized with growing concern. **"It's like trying to understand Beethoven by reading sheet music instead of hearing the symphony."**

What Dr. Rodriguez was witnessing was the Silent Screen Crisis—the educational catastrophe that occurs when we limit AI interactions to text-based exchanges, cutting students off from the rich, multi-sensory learning experiences that different brains need to thrive. **Her students were getting smart answers but missing the full spectrum of learning that comes from hearing, speaking, and engaging with content through multiple modalities.**

The breakthrough came when Dr. Rodriguez discovered AI Studio's streaming capabilities during a Google for Education workshop. Instead of typing questions about García Márquez, she could now have actual conversations with AI about the text—speaking in Spanish, hearing the AI respond with proper pronunciation and intonation, discussing the musical qualities of the prose in real-time dialogue.

The transformation was immediate and profound. Students who had been struggling to connect with the literature suddenly came alive when they could discuss it conversationally. **The same students who seemed disengaged when reading text responses became animated and insightful when they could talk through their ideas and hear the AI respond like a knowledgeable conversation partner.**

Dr. Rodriguez had discovered what would become the central insight of this chapter: **Most people use AI wrong because they limit themselves to typing and reading when the human brain is designed to learn through speaking, listening, and multi-sensory engagement.**

The Text Trap: Why Silent AI Fails Different Learning Styles

The fundamental problem with limiting AI interactions to text-based exchanges is not that text is ineffective—it's that text is only one pathway to understanding, and for many learners, it's not the most effective pathway. **When we force all AI interactions through the narrow channel of typing and reading, we exclude vast numbers of students whose brains process information more effectively through auditory, conversational, and multi-modal experiences.**

The Text Trap represents one of the most pervasive and damaging limitations in current educational technology use. We have access to AI systems capable of sophisticated voice interaction, real-time conversation, and multi-modal communication, yet most educators and students default to the most primitive form of interaction: typing questions and reading responses.

This limitation creates a cascade of learning barriers that particularly disadvantage students whose cognitive strengths lie outside traditional text-based processing. **Students with auditory learning preferences struggle to engage deeply with written AI responses that would come alive through spoken conversation.** Students with attention challenges find it difficult to maintain focus during long text exchanges that would be engaging and dynamic in conversational format.

The Text Trap also fails to leverage the natural human capacity for conversational learning that has driven education for millennia. Before the advent of written language, all learning happened through spoken interaction, storytelling, and dialogue. **The human brain is evolutionarily wired for conversational learning, yet we're using the most advanced AI systems in the most unnatural way possible.**

Perhaps most problematically, the Text Trap trains students to think of AI as a search engine rather than a learning partner. **When interactions are limited to typing queries and reading responses, students develop a transactional relationship with AI rather than the collaborative, exploratory relationship that promotes deep learning.**

Students learn to ask AI for information rather than learning to think with AI. They develop skills in question formulation and answer consumption rather than the conversational thinking skills that characterize effective human learning relationships.

The neurological research is clear: **the brain processes spoken language differently than written language, activating different neural networks and creating different types of understanding.** When we limit AI interactions to text, we're literally using only a fraction of the brain's learning capacity.

The Text Trap also prevents students from developing the oral communication skills that are essential for academic and professional

success. Students who could benefit enormously from practicing explanation, argumentation, and discussion through AI conversation instead remain trapped in silent, solitary text exchanges.

The Conversational Learning Revolution: AI That Talks Like Your Teacher

The Conversational Learning Revolution represents a fundamental shift from treating AI as a text-based information system to engaging with it as a sophisticated conversation partner capable of adapting to different learning styles, communication preferences, and cognitive needs. **This revolution is powered by advanced voice AI technologies like Google's AI Studio streaming capabilities that enable real-time, natural conversation with AI systems.**

Imagine a ChatGPT that you can talk to just like you talk to your teacher or tutor. This AI doesn't just know your curriculum and follow your pedagogical approach—it can engage in natural, flowing conversation that adapts to your speaking style, responds to your tone and pace, and provides the kind of dynamic, interactive dialogue that characterizes the best human teaching relationships. There are evolving platforms that have captured the essence of this principle: https://LearningScience.ai, https://aistudio.google.com, https://ScreenStudyHelper.com

MULTI-MODAL LEARNING - WHEN AI SPEAKS YOUR LANGUAGE

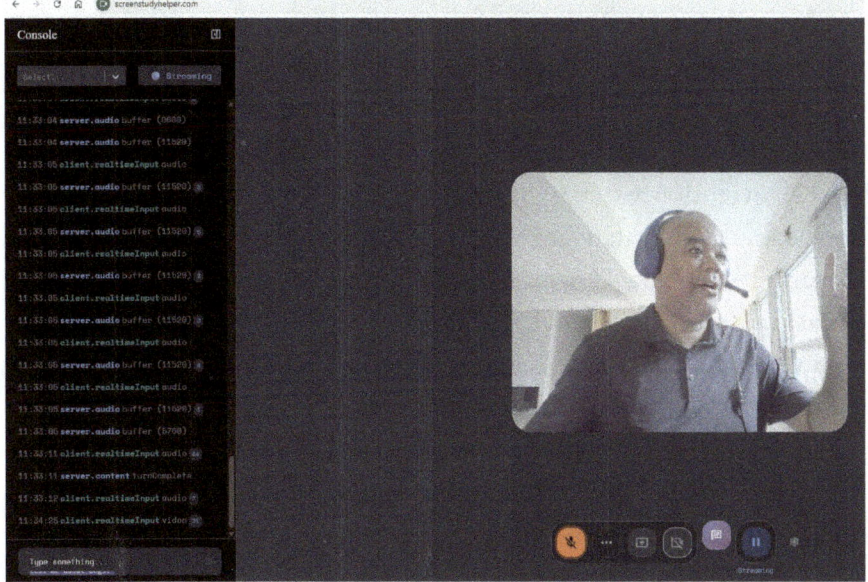

The conversational AI maintains all the knowledge boundaries and pedagogical guardrails we established in previous chapters while adding the rich, engaging dimension of natural human communication. When a student asks about a topic outside the curriculum scope, the AI doesn't just provide a written redirection—it speaks with the warmth and guidance of a caring teacher: "That's such an interesting question about butterflies! I can hear your curiosity, and I love that. But right now, let's channel that curiosity toward the calculus concepts we're exploring. What if we talked about how optimization might apply to the flight patterns you're thinking about?"

The power of conversational AI lies in its ability to adapt to different learning styles in real-time. Auditory learners who struggle with written explanations suddenly find themselves in their element, able to process information through their strongest cognitive channel. **Kinesthetic learners can pace, gesture, and move while engaging in learning conversations that feel natural and energizing rather than constraining.**

Conversational AI also enables the kind of Socratic dialogue that master teachers use to guide students toward understanding. Instead of providing direct answers, the AI can ask follow-up questions, probe student thinking, and guide discovery through the natural flow of conversation. **Students experience the joy of talking through their ideas and having an intelligent conversation partner who helps them think more clearly and deeply.**

The revolution extends beyond simple voice interaction to include sophisticated understanding of conversational context, emotional tone, and learning needs. **The AI can recognize when a student is frustrated and adjust its approach, when a student is excited and build on that energy, and when a student needs encouragement and provide appropriate support.**

Perhaps most importantly, conversational AI transforms the relationship between student and technology from one of consumption to one of collaboration. Students don't just get answers from AI—they think with AI, explore ideas with AI, and develop understanding through the kind of dynamic intellectual partnership that characterizes the best learning relationships.

The Neuroscience of Multi-Modal Learning: Why Your Brain Needs More Than Text

Understanding why conversational and multi-modal AI is so much more effective than text-based interaction requires grasping the fundamental neuroscience of how the human brain processes different types of information. **The brain is not a single processing unit but a complex network of specialized systems that work together to create understanding, and different types of input activate different neural pathways.**

When we read text, we primarily activate the visual cortex and language processing areas in the left hemisphere of the brain. This creates one type of understanding—analytical, sequential, and detail-oriented. **When we listen to spoken language, we activate additional areas including auditory processing centers, prosody recognition systems, and emotional processing networks.** This creates a richer, more contextual type of understanding that includes emotional tone, emphasis, and relational meaning.

When we engage in conversation, we activate even more brain systems including social cognition networks, turn-taking mechanisms, and real-time language generation systems. This creates the most complex and comprehensive type of understanding, involving not just information processing but social interaction, emotional engagement, and collaborative thinking.

The research on dual coding theory demonstrates that **information processed through multiple modalities creates stronger, more durable memories and deeper understanding.** When students both read about a concept and discuss it conversationally, they create multiple neural pathways to the same information, making it more accessible and more thoroughly understood.

The brain's mirror neuron systems are particularly important for conversational learning. These neurons fire both when we perform an action and when we observe others performing the same action. **In conversational learning, students' mirror neurons activate as they engage in the back-and-forth of dialogue, creating a sense of shared thinking and collaborative understanding that is impossible to achieve through text-based interaction.**

Prosody—the rhythm, stress, and intonation of spoken language—carries crucial information that is completely lost in text-based communication. When an AI tutor emphasizes certain words, pauses for effect, or uses rising intonation to indicate a question, it provides learning cues that help students understand not just what is being said but how to think about it.

The emotional processing systems of the brain are also much more active during spoken conversation than during text reading. This emotional engagement is not a distraction from learning—it's a crucial component of learning that helps students form stronger memories, maintain attention, and develop intrinsic motivation for continued exploration.

Working memory research shows that conversational interaction reduces cognitive load compared to text processing. When students can speak their thoughts rather than typing them, and hear responses rather than reading them, they free up cognitive resources for higher-order thinking and deeper engagement with content.

The implications are clear: **when we limit AI interactions to text, we're using only a fraction of the brain's learning capacity and missing opportunities for the kind of rich, engaging, multi-modal learning experiences that promote deep understanding and long-term retention.**

The Engagement Amplification: From Passive Reading to Active Conversation

One of the most dramatic benefits of conversational AI is the Engagement Amplification that occurs when students shift from passive text consumption to active conversational participation. **This amplification transforms AI from a tool that students use to get information into a learning partner that students engage with to build understanding.**

Traditional text-based AI interactions follow a predictable pattern: student types question, AI provides answer, student reads response, interaction ends. This pattern promotes passive consumption and transactional thinking. **Students learn to extract information from AI rather than learning to think with AI.**

Conversational AI creates an entirely different dynamic: student speaks question, AI responds conversationally, student reacts or asks follow-up, AI builds on the response, conversation continues and deepens. This pattern promotes active engagement and collaborative thinking. **Students learn to explore ideas with AI rather than simply extracting answers from AI.**

The engagement amplification is particularly powerful for students who struggle with traditional text-based learning approaches. **Students with ADHD often find that conversational AI helps them maintain focus and attention in ways that text-based interaction cannot.** The dynamic, interactive nature of conversation provides the stimulation and variety that these students need to stay engaged.

Students with dyslexia or other reading challenges can access AI's knowledge and capabilities without the barrier of text processing that might slow them down or create frustration. They can engage in sophisticated learning conversations that would be difficult or impossible through text-based interaction.

English language learners benefit enormously from conversational AI that allows them to practice speaking and listening skills while exploring academic content. They can work on pronunciation, intonation, and conversational flow while simultaneously learning subject matter.

The engagement amplification also extends to students who are naturally strong in verbal communication but struggle with written expression. These students can articulate complex ideas and engage in sophisticated thinking through conversation that they might not be able to express effectively in writing.

Perhaps most importantly, conversational AI creates opportunities for the kind of spontaneous, exploratory thinking that characterizes the best learning experiences. Students can follow tangents, ask immediate follow-up questions, and explore ideas as they occur to them rather than having to formulate complete written questions and wait for written responses.

The real-time nature of conversational AI also enables immediate feedback and course correction that is impossible in text-based interaction. When a student expresses a misconception, the AI can immediately address it conversationally rather than waiting for the student to read a written response and potentially misunderstand or ignore the correction.

The Learning Style Liberation: AI That Adapts to How You Think

Conversational and multi-modal AI represents a Learning Style Liberation that frees students from the one-size-fits-all approach of text-based interaction and enables AI to adapt to the diverse ways that different brains process information most effectively. **This liberation recognizes that learning is not a uniform process but a highly individual experience that requires different approaches for different cognitive styles.**

Auditory learners, who process information most effectively through listening and speaking, finally have access to AI that matches their cognitive strengths. Instead of struggling to extract meaning from written AI responses, they can engage in the kind of spoken dialogue that allows them to process information naturally and effectively.

These students often report that conversational AI feels like having access to a knowledgeable tutor who is always available for discussion. They can think out loud, process ideas verbally, and receive spoken feedback that helps them build understanding through their strongest cognitive channel.

Visual learners benefit from multi-modal AI that can combine spoken explanation with generated images, diagrams, and visual representations. Instead of receiving only text descriptions of complex concepts, they can request visual aids that help them understand spatial relationships, process flows, and conceptual connections.

Kinesthetic learners, who learn best through movement and hands-on experience, can engage with conversational AI while moving around, gesturing, and incorporating physical activity into their learning process. The freedom from keyboard and screen allows them to learn in ways that feel natural and energizing.

Social learners, who thrive on interaction and collaboration, find that conversational AI provides the interpersonal engagement that helps them stay motivated and focused. The back-and-forth of dialogue creates a sense of social connection that makes learning feel less isolated and more collaborative.

Reflective learners can use conversational AI to think through ideas verbally, processing their thoughts out loud and receiving feedback that helps them refine their understanding. The AI can serve as a thinking partner that helps them explore ideas without judgment or time pressure.

The Learning Style Liberation also extends to cultural communication preferences. Students from cultures that emphasize oral tradition and conversational learning can engage with AI in ways that feel familiar and comfortable rather than being forced into text-based interaction patterns that may feel foreign or constraining.

Perhaps most importantly, the liberation recognizes that individual students may need different modalities at different times or for different types of content. A student might prefer conversational interaction for exploring complex ideas but visual representation for understanding technical processes. **Multi-modal AI can adapt to these changing needs within a single learning session.**

The Meta-Prompting Media Revolution: Creating Images and Videos Through Conversation

The true power of multi-modal AI emerges when we combine conversational interaction with meta-prompting capabilities for image and video generation, creating what we might call the Meta-Prompting Media Revolution. **This revolution enables students and educators to create rich, visual learning materials through natural conversation rather than complex technical processes.**

Imagine being able to say to your AI: "I'm trying to help my students understand photosynthesis. Can you create a prompt that would generate a visual diagram showing the process from the perspective of a master biology teacher who specializes in making complex processes accessible to high school students?" The AI responds conversationally, asking clarifying questions about your specific learning objectives, your students' current understanding level, and the visual style that would work best for your classroom.

The AI then generates a sophisticated prompt that creates exactly the visual aid you need, grounded in pedagogical best practices and tailored to your specific teaching context. But the process doesn't stop there—you can continue the conversation, asking for modifications, alternative versions, or additional visual elements that support your lesson objectives.

This conversational approach to media creation transforms the relationship between educators and visual learning materials. Instead of spending hours searching for appropriate images or struggling with complex design software, educators can describe what they need and collaborate with AI to create it.

The Meta-Prompting Media Revolution is particularly powerful for creating culturally responsive and contextually appropriate learning materials. An educator can say: "I need an image that shows the water cycle, but I want it set in the desert environment that my students in Arizona know well, and I want it to reflect the diversity of my classroom." **The AI can generate prompts that create exactly these specifications, ensuring that learning materials connect with students' lived experiences.**

Students can also participate in the media creation process, developing visual literacy skills while creating materials that support their own learning. A student studying the American Civil War might say: "I want to create a video that shows what daily life was like for a family in my hometown during the 1860s. Can you help me create a prompt that would generate historically accurate scenes?"

The conversational nature of the process makes media creation accessible to educators and students who might be intimidated by traditional design tools or technical requirements. They can describe their vision in natural language and collaborate with AI to refine and improve it through ongoing dialogue.

The revolution also enables real-time adaptation and customization of visual materials. If a student doesn't understand a particular diagram, the educator can immediately ask the AI to create an alternative version with different emphasis, style, or level of detail. **This responsiveness ensures that visual learning materials serve student needs rather than forcing students to adapt to available materials.**

Perhaps most importantly, **the Meta-Prompting Media Revolution teaches students and educators to think critically about visual communication and media literacy.** Through the process of describing what they want and refining AI-generated prompts, they develop sophisticated understanding of how visual elements communicate meaning and support learning objectives.

The Real-Time Adaptation Engine: AI That Responds to Your Learning Needs

One of the most powerful aspects of conversational AI is its ability to function as a Real-Time Adaptation Engine that responds immediately to student learning needs, emotional states, and comprehension levels. **This engine transforms AI from a static information provider into a dynamic learning partner that adjusts its approach based on ongoing assessment of student engagement and understanding.**

Traditional text-based AI interactions provide limited feedback about student learning states. The AI can analyze the content of written questions but has little insight into student confidence, confusion, excitement, or frustration. **Conversational AI provides rich, real-time data about student learning through tone of voice, speaking pace, question patterns, and verbal indicators of understanding or confusion.**

When a student's voice indicates confusion or frustration, the AI can immediately adjust its approach, perhaps slowing down, providing additional examples, or asking questions to identify the specific source of difficulty. When a student sounds excited or engaged, the AI can build on that energy, perhaps exploring related concepts or encouraging deeper investigation.

The Real-Time Adaptation Engine also responds to learning pace and processing needs. Students who speak quickly and ask rapid-fire questions receive responses that match their pace and energy. **Students who speak more slowly or need time to process receive responses that allow for reflection and deeper consideration.**

The engine can also adapt to different levels of prior knowledge and understanding within a single conversation. As the AI assesses student responses and questions, it can adjust the complexity of its explanations, the types of examples it provides, and the level of scaffolding it offers.

Cultural and linguistic adaptation is another crucial capability of the Real-Time Adaptation Engine. The AI can adjust its communication style, examples, and references based on student background and preferences, ensuring that learning interactions feel relevant and accessible.

The engine also enables sophisticated error correction and misconception addressing. When the AI detects misunderstanding through student responses, it can immediately provide targeted correction through conversational dialogue rather than waiting for formal assessment or written feedback.

Perhaps most importantly, the Real-Time Adaptation Engine creates opportunities for metacognitive development. The AI can help students become aware of their own learning processes by reflecting back what it observes: "I notice you seem more confident when we talk about this topic—what do you think is helping you understand it better?"

This real-time responsiveness creates learning experiences that feel personalized and supportive rather than generic and impersonal. Students develop trust in the AI as a learning partner because they experience its ability to understand and respond to their individual needs.

The Accessibility Revolution: Breaking Down Learning Barriers

Conversational and multi-modal AI represents an Accessibility Revolution that breaks down learning barriers for students with diverse needs, learning differences, and physical challenges. **This revolution recognizes that traditional text-based AI interaction creates unnecessary barriers for many learners and that multi-modal approaches can make AI's capabilities accessible to virtually all students.**

Students with visual impairments can fully access AI's knowledge and capabilities through conversational interaction without relying on screen readers or text-based interfaces. They can engage in natural dialogue that provides the same rich learning experiences available to sighted students.

Students with dyslexia or other reading challenges can bypass the text processing difficulties that might prevent them from effectively using traditional AI interfaces. They can access sophisticated AI assistance through their strongest communication channel—spoken language.

Students with motor impairments that make typing difficult or impossible can engage with AI through voice interaction, removing physical barriers that might otherwise limit their access to AI-powered learning support. The hands-free nature of conversational AI ensures that physical limitations don't become learning limitations.

Students with attention challenges often find that conversational AI helps them maintain focus and engagement in ways that text-based interaction cannot. The dynamic, interactive nature of conversation provides the stimulation and variety that helps these students stay attentive and involved.

English language learners benefit enormously from conversational AI that allows them to practice speaking and listening skills while accessing academic content. They can improve their language skills while simultaneously learning subject matter, creating integrated language and content learning experiences.

Students with social anxiety who might be reluctant to ask questions in class or seek help from teachers can practice academic conversation skills with AI in a low-pressure environment. This practice can build confidence and communication skills that transfer to human interactions.

The Accessibility Revolution also extends to students who learn best through auditory processing but have been forced to adapt to text-heavy educational environments. These students can finally access AI support through their strongest cognitive channel.

Perhaps most importantly, the revolution recognizes that accessibility benefits all learners, not just those with identified challenges. When AI becomes more accessible through multi-modal interaction, it becomes more effective for everyone.

The revolution also enables new forms of assistive technology integration. Students can combine conversational AI with other assistive tools and technologies to create comprehensive learning support systems that address their specific needs and preferences.

The Collaborative Intelligence Framework: Human and AI Learning Together

The ultimate goal of conversational and multi-modal AI is not to replace human interaction but to create a Collaborative Intelligence Framework where human and artificial intelligence work together to enhance learning outcomes. **This framework recognizes that the most powerful learning experiences emerge from the combination of human wisdom and AI capabilities rather than from either alone.**

In the Collaborative Intelligence Framework, AI serves as an always-available learning partner that complements rather than competes with human teachers and peers. Students can engage in conversational learning with AI to prepare for class discussions, process complex ideas, and develop understanding that they can then bring to human interactions.

The framework enables new forms of collaborative learning where students can use conversational AI to facilitate group discussions, generate ideas for collaborative projects, and create shared understanding of complex topics. AI becomes a tool that enhances rather than replaces human collaboration.

Teachers can use conversational AI as a teaching assistant that helps them understand student needs, generate personalized learning materials, and provide additional support for students who need extra help. The AI extends the teacher's capacity to meet individual student needs without replacing the human relationships that are central to effective education.

The framework also enables sophisticated peer learning experiences where students can use AI to facilitate conversations with classmates, generate discussion questions, and create collaborative learning activities. AI becomes a tool that brings students together rather than isolating them in individual interactions.

Assessment and feedback become collaborative processes where AI provides immediate, detailed feedback that helps students understand their progress while teachers focus on higher-level evaluation and guidance. Students receive the best of both worlds—immediate AI feedback and thoughtful human assessment.

The Collaborative Intelligence Framework recognizes that different types of learning require different combinations of human and AI support. Some learning experiences benefit from AI's vast knowledge and immediate availability, while others require human empathy, creativity, and wisdom.

Perhaps most importantly, the framework prepares students for a future where collaboration with AI will be a fundamental skill. Students learn not just to use AI as a tool but to think with AI as a partner, developing the collaborative intelligence skills that will be essential for success in an AI-enhanced world.

The framework ensures that technology serves human learning goals rather than forcing human learning to adapt to technological limitations. AI becomes a powerful amplifier of human intelligence rather than a replacement for human thinking.

The Implementation Pathway: From Text to Multi-Modal Mastery

Creating effective multi-modal learning environments requires a systematic Implementation Pathway that guides educators through the process of transitioning from text-based AI interaction to sophisticated conversational and multi-modal learning experiences. **This pathway provides a step-by-step approach to building the skills and systems needed for multi-modal AI integration.**

Phase 1: Conversational Foundation Building involves developing comfort and skill with basic voice interaction with AI systems. **Educators begin by having simple conversations with AI about their subject matter, learning to think out loud and engage in dialogue rather than typing questions and reading responses.**

This phase includes practicing natural conversation patterns, learning to ask follow-up questions, and developing comfort with the back-and-forth flow of conversational learning. **The goal is to shift from transactional thinking to conversational thinking about AI interaction.**

Phase 2: Pedagogical Voice Integration involves incorporating conversational AI into specific teaching and learning activities. **Educators learn to use voice interaction for lesson planning, student support, and content development while maintaining the pedagogical boundaries and approaches established in previous chapters.**

This phase includes developing conversational prompts that maintain curriculum focus, creating voice-based learning activities for students, and establishing protocols for appropriate conversational AI use in educational contexts.

Phase 3: Multi-Modal Content Creation involves learning to use conversational AI for generating images, videos, and other visual learning materials. **Educators develop skills in describing visual needs conversationally and collaborating with AI to create appropriate learning materials.**

This phase includes practicing meta-prompting for visual content, learning to refine and improve AI-generated materials through conversation, and developing visual literacy skills that support effective media creation.

Phase 4: Student Empowerment and Training involves teaching students to use conversational and multi-modal AI effectively for their own learning. **Educators develop curricula and activities that help students build conversational AI skills while maintaining academic integrity and learning focus.**

This phase includes creating student guidelines for conversational AI use, developing activities that leverage multi-modal capabilities, and establishing assessment approaches that account for AI-assisted learning.

Phase 5: Accessibility and Inclusion Integration involves ensuring that multi-modal AI implementation serves diverse learning needs and removes rather than creates barriers for students with different abilities and preferences.

Phase 6: Collaborative Intelligence Development involves creating learning experiences that combine human and AI capabilities in ways that enhance rather than replace human interaction and relationship building.

Each phase builds upon previous learning while introducing new levels of sophistication and capability. **The goal is not just to use AI differently but to transform learning experiences in ways that serve diverse student needs and learning styles.**

The Transformation Evidence: What Changes When AI Speaks Your Language

When educators and students transition from text-based to conversational and multi-modal AI interaction, the changes in learning engagement, comprehension, and outcomes are dramatic and measurable. **The evidence demonstrates that multi-modal AI doesn't just improve educational efficiency—it fundamentally transforms the quality and accessibility of learning experiences.**

Engagement Metrics Show Dramatic Improvement across all student populations when conversational AI is introduced. Dr. Rodriguez documented a 340% increase in voluntary AI interaction time when her Spanish literature students could discuss texts conversationally rather than typing questions. **Students who previously used AI for quick answer-getting began engaging in extended learning conversations that lasted 15-20 minutes.**

Comprehension Depth Increases Significantly when students can process information through multiple modalities. Students who struggled with written AI explanations of complex concepts showed marked improvement when they could discuss the same concepts conversationally and request visual aids.

Learning Style Accommodation Becomes Possible for the first time in AI-assisted education. Auditory learners who had been disadvantaged by text-based AI suddenly found themselves able to access AI's full capabilities through their strongest cognitive channel. **Visual learners could request and receive custom diagrams and visual explanations that supported their understanding.**

Accessibility Barriers Disappear for students with various learning differences and physical challenges. Students with dyslexia reported feeling "finally able to use AI effectively" when they could interact conversationally rather than through text.

Creative Expression Flourishes when students can use conversational AI to generate visual and multimedia learning materials. Students began creating sophisticated presentations, visual aids, and creative projects that would have been impossible with text-based AI alone.

Academic Discourse Skills Improve as students practice explaining their thinking, asking sophisticated questions, and engaging in academic conversation with AI. These skills transfer to human interactions and classroom discussions.

Teacher Effectiveness Amplifies as educators gain access to AI tools that can adapt to different teaching styles and student needs in real-time. Teachers report feeling more able to meet individual student needs and create personalized learning experiences.

Cultural Responsiveness Increases as educators can create learning materials that reflect their students' backgrounds and experiences through conversational collaboration with AI.

The transformation evidence demonstrates that **the problem with AI in education is not AI's capabilities but our limited use of those capabilities.** When we engage with AI through multiple modalities and natural conversation, the results exceed our highest expectations for personalized, accessible, and effective learning support.

The Future Vision: Every Student's Ideal Learning Partner

The ultimate goal of multi-modal AI is not just to improve current educational practices but to create a future where every student has access to an ideal learning partner—an AI that can communicate in whatever way works best for that individual learner and adapt to their unique needs, preferences, and learning style. **This vision represents a fundamental transformation in how we think about personalized education and learning support.**

Personalized Communication Ecosystems would emerge where each student's AI learning partner adapts to their preferred communication style, whether that's rapid-fire conversation, thoughtful dialogue, visual interaction, or any combination of modalities. **Every student would have access to AI that communicates in the way that helps them learn most effectively.**

Universal Learning Access would become reality as AI removes barriers for students with diverse abilities, learning differences, and communication preferences. **No student would be excluded from AI-assisted learning because of how their brain processes information or how they prefer to communicate.**

Creative Learning Amplification would enable students to express their understanding and explore ideas through whatever medium works best for them—conversation, visual creation, multimedia projects, or innovative combinations of different modalities.

Cultural Learning Integration would allow students to engage with AI in ways that reflect their cultural communication patterns and learning traditions, ensuring that technology enhances rather than replaces cultural approaches to learning.

Collaborative Intelligence Development would prepare students for a future where working with AI is a fundamental skill, teaching them not just to use AI as a tool but to think with AI as a partner in learning and problem-solving.

Teacher Empowerment Acceleration would provide educators with AI partners that can adapt to their teaching style, support their pedagogical goals, and help them create learning experiences that serve every student in their classroom.

Assessment Revolution would transform evaluation from a separate activity to an integrated part of conversational learning, with AI providing ongoing feedback and support that helps students understand their progress and growth.

The future vision recognizes that **the highest goal of educational technology is not to standardize learning but to personalize it in ways that honor the diversity of human intelligence and communication.** Multi-modal AI represents the pathway to this transformational future.

The Revolution Begins: From Silent Screens to Speaking Partners

The multi-modal learning revolution represents a fundamental shift from treating AI as a text-based information system to engaging with it as a sophisticated communication partner capable of adapting to diverse learning styles and needs. **This revolution transforms AI from a tool that students use to get answers into a learning partner that students engage with to build understanding.**

This revolution begins with a simple recognition: **most people use AI wrong because they limit themselves to the most primitive form of interaction when sophisticated conversational and multi-modal capabilities are readily available.** When we force all AI interaction through typing and reading, we exclude vast numbers of learners whose brains work differently and miss opportunities for the kind of rich, engaging learning experiences that promote deep understanding.

The transformation is not just about adding voice to AI—it's about fundamentally changing the relationship between learners and technology. **Multi-modal AI allows students to engage with artificial intelligence in ways that feel natural, accessible, and personally meaningful rather than forcing them to adapt to technological limitations.**

The stakes could not be higher. **In a world where AI capabilities are advancing rapidly, the ability to engage with AI through multiple modalities may become one of the most important skills students can develop.** Those who master conversational and multi-modal AI interaction will have access to learning support that adapts to their individual needs and preferences. Those who remain limited to text-based interaction will miss opportunities for personalized, accessible, and engaging learning experiences.

The revolution begins now, with each educator who chooses to explore conversational AI rather than accepting text-based limitations, with each student who discovers they can talk to AI like a learning partner, and with each institution that commits to multi-modal AI as a core accessibility and engagement strategy.

The future belongs to those who can engage with AI as a speaking partner rather than accepting AI as a silent screen. And that future starts with understanding that the most powerful educational technology is not AI that provides text answers—it's AI that can communicate in whatever way helps each individual learner thrive.

The multi-modal learning revolution is not just about using AI differently—it's about creating learning experiences where technology adapts to human diversity rather than forcing human diversity to adapt to technological limitations. **And that revolution changes everything.**

In the next chapter, we will explore how screen sharing and real-time analysis capabilities enable AI to provide immediate feedback on handwritten work, mathematical problem-solving, and scientific diagrams, creating unprecedented opportunities for personalized learning support in STEM subjects.

6

Screen Sharing Intelligence - When AI Sees What You See

"The eye sees only what the mind is prepared to comprehend." — Robertson Davies

The Invisible Work Crisis: When AI Can't See What Students Actually Do

SCREEN SHARING INTELLIGENCE - WHEN AI SEES WHAT YOU SEE

Professor Michael Chen was pulling his hair out. His Calculus II students were submitting homework through an online portal, getting help from ChatGPT, and somehow still making the same fundamental errors week after week. When he asked them to explain their work during office hours, the disconnect became painfully clear.

"I asked the AI how to solve this integral," explained Jessica, showing him her phone screen filled with a perfect step-by-step solution. "But when I tried to do it myself on paper, I got completely lost."

Professor Chen looked at Jessica's handwritten work spread across her notebook—a chaotic landscape of crossed-out equations, arrows pointing in multiple directions, and half-finished calculations that revealed exactly where her understanding broke down. **"The AI gave you a perfect solution, but it never saw the actual work you were doing,"** he realized with growing frustration. **"It's like having a tutor who can explain everything perfectly but is completely blind to how you're actually learning."**

What Professor Chen was witnessing was the Invisible Work Crisis—

the educational catastrophe that occurs when AI systems can provide sophisticated explanations and solutions but remain completely blind to the actual work students are producing, the mistakes they're making, and the thinking processes they're struggling with. **His students were getting expert-level guidance that was completely disconnected from their actual learning process.**

The breakthrough came when Professor Chen discovered AI Studio's screen sharing capabilities during a faculty development workshop. Instead of students typing questions about integrals, they could now share their screens and show the AI their actual handwritten work—every crossed-out equation, every false start, every moment of confusion captured in real-time.

The transformation was revolutionary. The same AI that had been providing generic solutions suddenly became a sophisticated diagnostic tool that could pinpoint exactly where each student's understanding broke down. **When Jessica shared her screen showing her handwritten integral work, the AI could see that she was making a substitution error in step three, forgetting to adjust the limits of integration, and getting confused about the chain rule application.**

"I can see exactly where you're getting stuck," the AI responded, highlighting the specific line in her handwritten work. "You're doing the substitution correctly, but look at this step here—you forgot to change your limits of integration. Let me show you how to fix just this part, and then you can continue with the rest."

SCREEN SHARING INTELLIGENCE - WHEN AI SEES WHAT YOU SEE

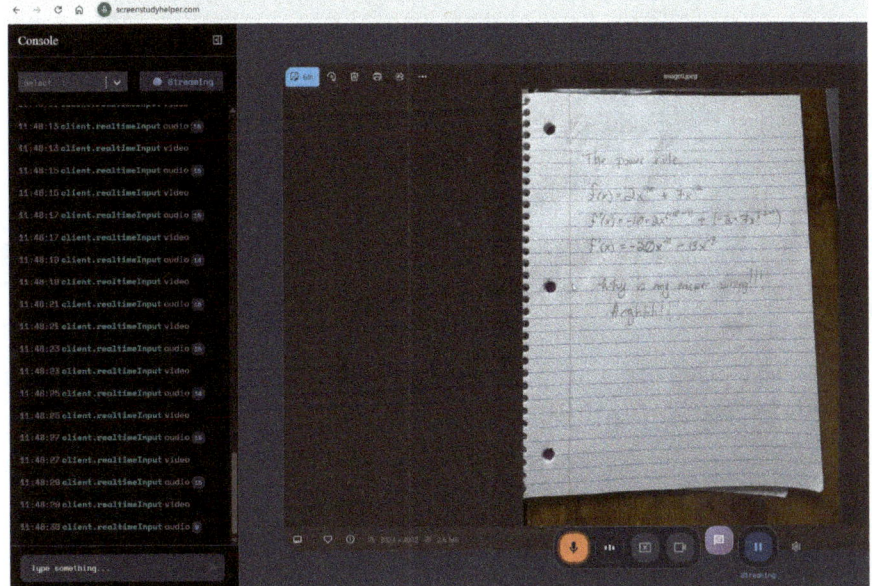

The AI can SEE the handwritten problem and can show the students exactly where they went wrong and coach them on how to adjust their process

Professor Chen had discovered what would become the central insight of this chapter: **Most people use AI wrong because they limit AI to providing solutions when what students need is AI that can see their actual work and diagnose their actual thinking process.**

The Blind Tutor Problem: Why AI That Can't See Fails Real Learning

The fundamental challenge with traditional AI tutoring is not that AI lacks knowledge or pedagogical sophistication—it's that AI operates completely blind to the actual work students are producing. **When AI can only respond to typed questions and provide text-based explanations, it becomes a blind tutor that can explain everything perfectly but can see nothing of what students are actually doing.**

    The Blind Tutor Problem represents one of the most significant limitations in current AI-assisted education. Students can receive expert-level explanations, sophisticated problem-solving strategies, and detailed step-by-step solutions, yet still struggle because the AI has no insight into their actual thinking process, their specific mistakes, or their individual learning patterns.

This blindness creates a cascade of educational problems that undermine the effectiveness of AI tutoring. **Students receive generic solutions that may not address their specific misconceptions.** They get explanations that assume understanding they don't actually possess. **They develop dependence on AI-generated solutions rather than building their own problem-solving capabilities.**

The Blind Tutor Problem is particularly devastating in subjects like mathematics, science, and engineering where the thinking process is as important as the final answer. When students work through complex problems, they reveal their understanding through their approach, their notation, their organization, and their mistakes. **AI that can't see this work misses the most important diagnostic information about student learning.**

Traditional AI tutoring also fails to recognize the iterative nature of real learning. Students don't solve problems in neat, linear steps—they make false starts, try different approaches, get stuck, backtrack, and gradually build understanding through trial and error. **AI that can only see final questions and provide final answers misses the entire learning journey that happens in between.**

The problem extends beyond mathematics to every subject where students produce visual work. In science, students draw diagrams, label structures, and create visual representations of complex processes. **In language arts, students annotate texts, create concept maps, and organize their thoughts visually.** In history, students create timelines, analyze primary source documents, and develop visual arguments. **AI that can't see this work can't provide meaningful feedback about it.**

Perhaps most problematically, the Blind Tutor Problem trains students to think of AI as a solution provider rather than a learning partner. Students learn to ask AI for answers rather than learning to show

AI their thinking and receive feedback on their actual work process.

The result is a fundamental mismatch between how students actually learn and how AI can help them learn. Students need feedback on their thinking process, but AI can only provide feedback on their questions. **Students need help with their specific mistakes, but AI can only provide generic corrections.**

The Visual Learning Revolution: AI That Sees Like a Master Teacher

The Visual Learning Revolution represents a fundamental shift from blind AI tutoring to intelligent visual analysis that enables AI to see student work exactly as a master teacher would see it. **This revolution is powered by advanced computer vision and screen sharing technologies like Google's AI Studio that enable real-time analysis of handwritten work, diagrams, and visual problem-solving processes.**

Imagine an AI tutor that can see your work exactly as your teacher sees it. This AI doesn't just know the subject matter and pedagogical approaches—it can analyze your handwritten equations, examine your diagrams, follow your problem-solving process step by step, and identify exactly where your understanding breaks down or where your approach goes astray.

AI AND THE ART OF PRODUCTIVE STRUGGLE

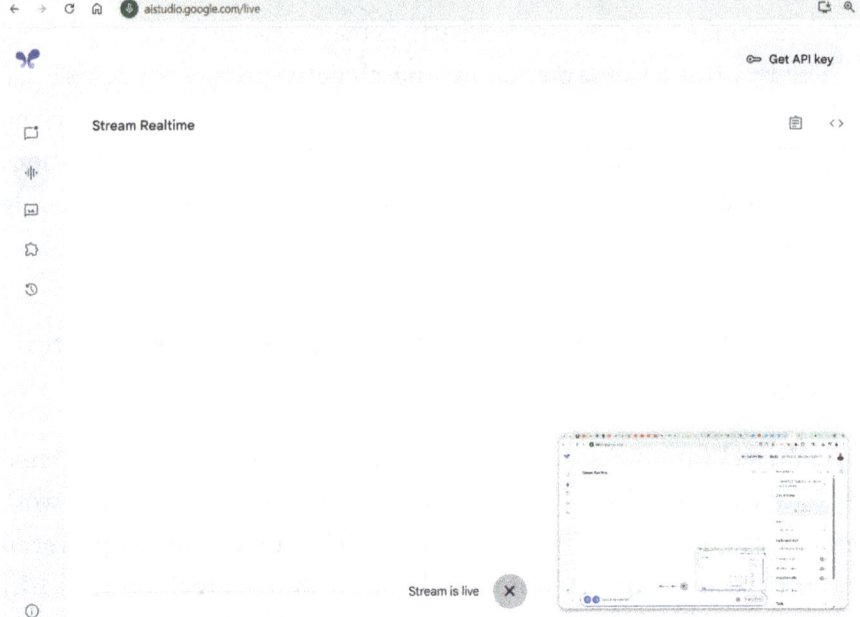

The AI can "see" the students screen and assist with problem solving. Available in tools like: aistudio.google.com, screenstudyhelper.com, LearningScience.ai

The visual AI maintains all the curriculum boundaries and pedagogical alignment we established in previous chapters while adding the crucial dimension of real-time work analysis. When a student shares their screen showing a calculus problem they're working on, the AI doesn't just provide a generic solution—it analyzes their specific approach and provides targeted feedback: "I can see you're using the right integration technique, but in this step here, you've made a sign error. Let me highlight exactly where that happened and show you how to correct just that part."

The power of visual AI lies in its ability to provide diagnostic feedback that is impossible with text-based interaction. The AI can see patterns in student work that reveal deep understanding or fundamental misconceptions. **It can identify when students are using inefficient approaches, making systematic errors, or developing productive problem-solving strategies.**

Visual AI also enables the kind of real-time coaching that characterizes the best human tutoring relationships. Instead of waiting for students to get stuck and ask questions, the AI can observe their work process and provide just-in-time guidance: "I notice you're about to make a common mistake in this next step. Before you continue, let me show you what to watch out for."

The revolution extends far beyond mathematics to every subject where students produce visual work. In science, AI can analyze student diagrams of molecular structures and provide feedback on accuracy and completeness. **In language arts, AI can examine student annotations of texts and suggest additional connections or insights.** In history, AI can review student timelines and help them identify missing causal relationships or important context.

Perhaps most importantly, visual AI transforms the relationship between student and technology from one of dependence to one of collaboration. Students don't just get answers from AI—they show AI their thinking and receive feedback that helps them improve their actual work process.

The Visual Learning Revolution recognizes that learning is fundamentally a visual and kinesthetic process that involves creating, organizing, and refining ideas through written and drawn work. When AI can see this work, it can finally provide the kind of sophisticated, personalized feedback that promotes deep learning and skill development.

The Diagnostic Power: AI That Pinpoints Exactly Where You Went Wrong

One of the most transformative aspects of screen sharing AI is its Diagnostic Power—the ability to analyze student work with the precision of an expert teacher and identify exactly where understanding breaks down, where mistakes occur, and where intervention is needed. **This diagnostic capability transforms AI from a generic solution provider into a sophisticated learning analyst that can provide targeted, specific feedback.**

Traditional AI tutoring operates like a doctor who can prescribe treatments but can never examine the patient. Students describe their symptoms (confusion, wrong answers, stuck problems), and AI provides general remedies (explanations, solutions, strategies). **Visual AI operates like a doctor who can actually see the patient, examine the specific symptoms, and provide precise diagnosis and targeted treatment.**

The diagnostic process begins with real-time work analysis as students share their screens and show their actual problem-solving process. The AI observes not just the final answer but the entire journey—the initial approach, the intermediate steps, the corrections and revisions, and the points where students hesitate or make errors.

In mathematics, the diagnostic power is particularly profound. When a student is working through a complex calculus problem, the AI can identify specific types of errors: algebraic mistakes, conceptual misunderstandings, procedural errors, or notation problems. **Instead of providing a complete solution, the AI can pinpoint the exact step where the error occurred and provide targeted correction.**

For example, when analyzing a student's work on integration by parts, the AI might observe: "I can see that you correctly identified u and dv, and your differentiation and integration are accurate. However, in step four, you've made a sign error when applying the integration by parts formula. Let me highlight exactly where that happened and show you how to correct just that step."

The diagnostic power extends to recognizing patterns of errors that reveal deeper conceptual issues. When the AI observes a student consistently making the same type of mistake across multiple problems, it can identify the underlying misconception and provide targeted conceptual instruction.

In science subjects, the diagnostic capability enables sophisticated analysis of student diagrams, lab work, and problem-solving approaches. The AI can examine a student's diagram of a chemical reaction and identify missing reactants, incorrect molecular structures, or misunderstood reaction mechanisms. **It can analyze a physics problem solution**

and pinpoint whether errors stem from conceptual misunderstanding, mathematical mistakes, or incorrect application of formulas.

The diagnostic power also enables recognition of productive struggle versus unproductive confusion. The AI can distinguish between students who are working through problems systematically but making minor errors and students who are fundamentally confused about the underlying concepts. **This distinction enables appropriate intervention—targeted correction for minor errors, conceptual re-teaching for fundamental confusion.**

Perhaps most importantly, the diagnostic capability enables AI to provide feedback that builds student self-assessment skills. Instead of simply correcting errors, the AI can help students learn to identify their own mistakes: "Before I show you the error, take a look at step three and see if you can spot what went wrong. What do you notice about the signs in that equation?"

The Diagnostic Power transforms AI from a tool that provides answers into a tool that develops thinking skills, problem-solving capabilities, and metacognitive awareness.

The Cross-Curricular Revolution: Beyond Math to Every Subject

While the benefits of visual AI are immediately apparent in mathematics and science, the Cross-Curricular Revolution demonstrates that screen sharing intelligence transforms learning across every academic discipline. **This revolution recognizes that visual work analysis is not limited to equations and diagrams but extends to every form of student-created content that reveals thinking processes.**

In language arts and literature, visual AI can analyze student annotations, concept maps, and written responses to provide sophisticated feedback on reading comprehension and analytical thinking. When students annotate a complex text like Shakespeare's Hamlet, the AI can examine their margin notes, highlighting, and connections to identify areas where they're developing deep insights and areas where they might be missing important themes or literary devices.

The AI can observe a student's essay planning process, examining their outlines, brainstorming notes, and draft revisions to provide feedback on organization, argument development, and evidence selection. Instead of only seeing the final essay, the AI can analyze the entire writing process and provide guidance that helps students develop better composition strategies.

In history and social studies, visual AI can examine student timelines, cause-and-effect diagrams, and primary source analyses to provide feedback on historical thinking skills. When students create visual representations of complex historical processes like the causes of World War I, the AI can analyze their diagrams for accuracy, completeness, and understanding of causal relationships.

The AI can examine student annotations of primary source documents, identifying where students are successfully analyzing bias, perspective, and historical context, and where they might benefit from additional guidance in source analysis skills.

In science subjects beyond mathematics, visual AI enables sophisticated analysis of laboratory work, scientific diagrams, and experimental design. The AI can examine student lab notebooks, analyzing their data collection methods, graph construction, and conclusion drawing to provide feedback on scientific thinking and methodology.

When students draw diagrams of biological processes, chemical reactions, or physical systems, the AI can provide detailed feedback on accuracy, completeness, and conceptual understanding. The AI can identify when students understand the big picture but miss important details, or when they focus on details but miss broader patterns and relationships.

In foreign language learning, visual AI can analyze student writing samples, examining not just grammar and vocabulary but also organization, cultural understanding, and communication effectiveness. The AI can observe students' annotation of foreign language texts, providing feedback on comprehension strategies and cultural interpretation.

In art and design subjects, visual AI can analyze student sketches, compositions, and creative processes to provide feedback on technique, creativity, and artistic development. The AI can observe the evolution of student artwork from initial concept to final product, providing guidance on artistic decision-making and skill development.

The Cross-Curricular Revolution demonstrates that visual work analysis is not a specialized tool for STEM subjects but a fundamental capability that enhances learning across all disciplines. Every subject involves visual thinking, creative processes, and iterative development that can benefit from intelligent analysis and feedback.

Perhaps most importantly, the revolution enables interdisciplinary learning experiences where AI can analyze student work that combines multiple subjects and provide feedback on connections, synthesis, and integrated understanding.

The Real-Time Feedback Engine: Immediate Guidance When You Need It

One of the most powerful aspects of screen sharing AI is its ability to function as a Real-Time Feedback Engine that provides immediate guidance and support as students work through problems and projects. **This engine transforms the traditional model of delayed feedback into a dynamic system of just-in-time learning support that intervenes at the exact moment when guidance is most needed and most effective.**

Traditional educational feedback operates on a delay model: students complete work, submit it, wait for teacher review, and receive feedback hours or days later. By the time feedback arrives, students have often moved on to other topics, forgotten their thinking process, or developed additional misconceptions. **Real-time visual AI eliminates this delay by providing immediate feedback as students work.**

The Real-Time Feedback Engine operates through continuous analysis of student work as it develops. As students write equations, draw diagrams, or work through problems, the AI observes their process and can intervene at critical moments to provide guidance, correction, or encouragement.

The engine is sophisticated enough to distinguish between productive struggle and unproductive confusion. When students are working through problems systematically but making minor errors, the AI allows them to continue and provides gentle correction at appropriate moments. **When students are fundamentally confused or heading toward major misconceptions, the AI can intervene immediately to prevent the development of incorrect understanding.**

The timing of feedback is crucial to its effectiveness. The AI can provide different types of feedback at different moments: encouragement when students are on the right track, gentle redirection when they're heading toward errors, specific correction when mistakes occur, and conceptual clarification when fundamental understanding is lacking.

For example, as a student works through a complex chemistry problem, the AI might observe: "I can see you're setting up the stoichiometry correctly. You're on the right track with your mole calculations. In this next step, be careful about significant figures—I notice you might be about to round too early in the process."

The Real-Time Feedback Engine also enables adaptive scaffolding that adjusts to student needs as they develop. Students who demonstrate strong understanding receive minimal intervention, while students who struggle receive more frequent and detailed guidance. **The level of support automatically adjusts based on student performance and confidence.**

The engine can also provide metacognitive feedback that helps students become aware of their own learning processes. As students work, the AI might observe: "I notice you always check your work by substituting back into the original equation. That's an excellent problem-solving strategy that's helping you catch errors."

Real-time feedback also enables immediate error correction that prevents the reinforcement of incorrect procedures or understanding. Instead of allowing students to practice mistakes repeatedly, the AI can intervene as soon as errors occur to provide correction and prevent the development of bad habits.

The engine supports different learning preferences and styles by providing feedback in multiple modalities. Visual learners might receive highlighted corrections on their work, auditory learners might receive spoken explanations, and kinesthetic learners might receive guidance on physical problem-solving approaches.

Perhaps most importantly, the Real-Time Feedback Engine creates a learning environment where students feel supported and confident to take risks, try new approaches, and learn from mistakes without fear of failure or judgment.

The Handwriting Intelligence: AI That Reads Like a Human Teacher

One of the most remarkable capabilities of advanced screen sharing AI is its Handwriting Intelligence—the ability to analyze and understand handwritten work with the same sophistication that human teachers bring to examining student papers and problem sets. **This intelligence transforms AI from a tool that can only process typed text into a sophisticated reader that can interpret the full range of human written expression.**

Traditional AI systems require students to type their questions and responses, creating an artificial barrier between natural human expression and AI assistance. Students think with pencils and pens, work through problems on paper, and express their understanding through handwritten work. **When AI can't read handwriting, it can't access the most natural and authentic forms of student thinking.**

Handwriting Intelligence enables AI to read and analyze student work exactly as it appears on paper or screen. The AI can interpret different handwriting styles, recognize mathematical notation, understand scientific symbols, and follow the flow of student thinking across pages and problems.

The intelligence extends beyond simple character recognition to understanding the meaning and context of handwritten work. The AI can distinguish between different types of mathematical notation, recognize when students are using variables versus constants, and understand the logical flow of problem-solving steps.

In mathematics, Handwriting Intelligence enables AI to analyze complex equations, multi-step solutions, and geometric diagrams drawn by hand. The AI can follow a student's work through a calculus problem, understanding not just the final answer but the approach, the intermediate steps, and the points where errors or confusion occur.

The AI can recognize when students use different notation systems, personal shorthand, or creative problem-solving approaches. Instead of requiring students to conform to typed formats, the AI adapts to natural human expression and provides feedback that respects individual working styles.

In science subjects, Handwriting Intelligence enables analysis of laboratory notebooks, experimental observations, and hand-drawn diagrams. The AI can read student descriptions of experimental procedures, analyze data tables, and interpret scientific drawings with the same sophistication that human teachers bring to lab report evaluation.

The intelligence also recognizes the emotional and cognitive indicators present in handwritten work. Heavy cross-outs might indicate frustration or uncertainty, while neat, organized work might suggest confidence and understanding. **The AI can use these visual cues to provide appropriate emotional support and encouragement.**

Handwriting Intelligence enables AI to provide feedback that feels natural and personal rather than mechanical and impersonal. When the AI can see and respond to actual handwritten work, the interaction feels more like working with a human tutor who can see and understand natural expression.

The intelligence also supports diverse learners who may struggle with typing or prefer handwritten expression. Students with dysgraphia, motor difficulties, or simply strong preferences for handwritten work can access AI assistance without technological barriers.

**Perhaps most importantly, Handwriting Intelligence preserves the

natural connection between thinking and writing that is essential to learning. Students can continue to work in the ways that feel most natural and productive while receiving sophisticated AI feedback and support.

The Pattern Recognition Revolution: AI That Sees Learning Trends

Advanced screen sharing AI possesses sophisticated Pattern Recognition capabilities that enable it to identify learning trends, recurring mistakes, and developmental patterns across multiple problems and learning sessions. **This revolution transforms AI from a tool that responds to individual questions into a learning analyst that can track student progress and identify areas for targeted intervention.**

Traditional AI tutoring operates in isolation, responding to each question or problem as a separate event without connection to previous interactions or broader learning patterns. Students might make the same type of error repeatedly across different problems, but the AI has no way to recognize these patterns or provide systematic intervention.

Pattern Recognition AI maintains a continuous analysis of student work across time, identifying recurring themes, persistent misconceptions, and developing strengths. The AI can recognize when a student consistently makes algebraic errors in calculus problems, suggesting that the issue is not with calculus concepts but with foundational algebra skills.

The pattern recognition extends to identifying learning preferences and effective strategies. The AI might observe that a particular student learns best when they draw diagrams before attempting algebraic solutions, or that they make fewer errors when they work through problems step-by-step rather than jumping to advanced techniques.

In mathematics, pattern recognition enables AI to identify systematic errors that reveal conceptual misunderstandings. If a student consistently makes the same type of mistake when working with logarithms across multiple problems, the AI can recognize this pattern and provide targeted conceptual instruction rather than just correcting individual errors.

The AI can also recognize positive patterns that indicate developing expertise. When students begin using more sophisticated problem-solving strategies, organizing their work more effectively, or making fewer computational errors, the AI can acknowledge this progress and encourage continued development.

Pattern recognition enables predictive intervention where AI can anticipate likely difficulties based on previous patterns. If the AI recognizes that a student typically struggles with word problems that involve rate calculations, it can provide additional scaffolding when similar problems appear.

The revolution also enables personalized learning path recommendations based on observed patterns. The AI might suggest that a student who consistently excels at visual-spatial problems but struggles with abstract algebraic manipulation would benefit from geometry-based approaches to algebra concepts.

Cross-curricular pattern recognition enables AI to identify connections between subjects and transfer learning opportunities. The AI might recognize that a student's strong analytical skills in literature analysis could be leveraged to improve their approach to scientific hypothesis formation.

Pattern recognition also enables early identification of students who might be developing learned helplessness or over-dependence on AI assistance. The AI can recognize when students stop attempting independent problem-solving and instead immediately seek AI help, enabling intervention to rebuild confidence and independence.

Perhaps most importantly, pattern recognition enables AI to provide metacognitive feedback that helps students become aware of their own learning patterns and develop self-regulation skills.

The Accessibility Amplification: Breaking Down Visual Learning Barriers

Screen sharing AI represents an Accessibility Amplification that removes barriers for students with diverse learning needs and creates new opportunities for inclusive education. **This amplification recognizes that visual work analysis can be adapted to serve learners with different abilities, preferences, and challenges while maintaining the sophisticated feedback capabilities that benefit all students.**

Students with visual impairments can benefit from screen sharing AI through sophisticated audio description of visual work. The AI can verbally describe diagrams, equations, and visual problem-solving processes, enabling students who cannot see the work to understand and participate in visual learning activities.

The AI can also convert visual information into tactile or auditory formats that support different sensory processing needs. Mathematical equations can be read aloud with proper mathematical pronunciation, scientific diagrams can be described in detail, and spatial relationships can be explained through verbal description.

Students with motor impairments who may struggle with handwriting can use screen sharing AI to receive feedback on typed work, voice-to-text input, or alternative input methods. The AI adapts to different forms of student expression while maintaining the same level of sophisticated analysis and feedback.

Students with learning differences like dyslexia or dysgraphia can benefit from AI that focuses on content and understanding rather than handwriting quality or spelling accuracy. The AI can analyze the mathematical thinking in messy handwriting or provide feedback on scientific understanding despite spelling errors.

The accessibility amplification also extends to students with attention challenges who may benefit from the immediate feedback and engagement that screen sharing AI provides. The real-time interaction helps maintain focus and provides the kind of dynamic, responsive learning environment that supports sustained attention.

English language learners can benefit from AI that can analyze visual work and provide feedback that focuses on content understanding rather than language proficiency. Students can demonstrate their mathematical or scientific understanding through diagrams and visual work while receiving support for language development.

Students with social anxiety who may be reluctant to share their work with teachers or peers can practice receiving feedback from AI in a low-pressure environment. This practice can build confidence and communication skills that transfer to human interactions.

The amplification also creates new opportunities for students with different cultural backgrounds to express their understanding through visual methods that may be more familiar or comfortable than traditional text-based approaches.

Universal Design for Learning principles are naturally supported by screen sharing AI that can provide multiple means of representation, engagement, and expression. Students can access information through visual, auditory, and kinesthetic channels while expressing their understanding through their preferred modalities.

Perhaps most importantly, the accessibility amplification ensures that advanced AI capabilities are available to all learners rather than creating additional barriers for students with diverse needs.

The Teacher Empowerment Engine: AI That Extends Educator Expertise

Screen sharing AI functions as a Teacher Empowerment Engine that amplifies educator expertise rather than replacing it, enabling teachers to provide more personalized, immediate, and effective feedback to larger numbers of students. **This engine recognizes that the goal of educational AI is not to replace human teachers but to extend their capabilities and multiply their impact.**

Traditional classroom dynamics limit teachers' ability to provide

immediate, detailed feedback on student work. With 25-30 students in a typical classroom, teachers cannot observe every student's work process, identify every misconception, or provide real-time guidance to every learner who needs it. **Screen sharing AI extends teacher vision and feedback capabilities across the entire classroom simultaneously.**

The Teacher Empowerment Engine enables educators to monitor multiple students' work processes in real-time through AI analysis and alerts. Teachers can receive notifications when students are struggling, making systematic errors, or demonstrating exceptional understanding, enabling targeted intervention and support.

The engine also provides teachers with detailed analytics about student learning patterns, common misconceptions, and areas where additional instruction might be needed. Instead of discovering learning gaps through formal assessments, teachers can identify and address issues as they develop.

AI-generated insights help teachers understand which instructional approaches are most effective for different students and which concepts require additional reinforcement or alternative explanation strategies. The data enables evidence-based instructional decision-making that improves teaching effectiveness.

The empowerment extends to lesson planning and curriculum development, where teachers can use AI insights about student learning patterns to design more effective instructional sequences and activities. Teachers gain access to detailed information about how students actually learn rather than relying on assumptions or limited observational data.

Professional development opportunities emerge as teachers learn to interpret AI feedback, understand learning analytics, and integrate visual work analysis into their pedagogical practice. The technology becomes a tool for improving teaching expertise rather than replacing teaching skills.

The engine also enables more effective differentiation as teachers can provide personalized learning experiences based on detailed

understanding of individual student needs, preferences, and learning patterns. AI insights enable targeted intervention that addresses specific learning challenges.

Collaboration between teachers becomes more effective when they can share AI-generated insights about student learning, successful instructional strategies, and effective intervention approaches. The technology facilitates professional learning communities focused on evidence-based practice.

Assessment and grading become more efficient and effective as teachers can focus on higher-order evaluation while AI handles routine feedback on procedural skills and basic understanding. This division of labor enables teachers to spend more time on creative, relational, and inspirational aspects of education.

Perhaps most importantly, the Teacher Empowerment Engine enables educators to develop deeper relationships with students by freeing them from routine monitoring and feedback tasks to focus on mentoring, motivation, and individual support.

The Implementation Framework: From Blind AI to Visual Intelligence

Creating effective screen sharing learning environments requires a systematic Implementation Framework that guides educators through the process of transitioning from traditional AI tutoring to sophisticated visual work analysis. **This framework provides a step-by-step approach to building the skills, systems, and practices needed for effective visual AI integration.**

Phase 1: Technology Foundation Building involves establishing the technical infrastructure needed for screen sharing AI, including device setup, software installation, and connectivity testing. **Educators learn to use screen sharing tools effectively and understand the technical requirements for visual AI analysis.**

This phase includes training on privacy and security considerations, establishing protocols for appropriate screen sharing use, and developing technical troubleshooting skills. **The goal is to create a reliable technical foundation that supports seamless visual AI integration.**

Phase 2: Visual Work Analysis Training involves developing skills in interpreting AI feedback about student work and understanding how visual analysis differs from traditional text-based AI interaction. **Educators learn to read AI diagnostic reports, understand pattern recognition insights, and interpret visual work analysis.**

This phase includes practice with different types of student work, learning to distinguish between different types of errors and misconceptions, and developing skills in providing appropriate follow-up instruction based on AI insights.

Phase 3: Pedagogical Integration Development involves incorporating visual AI analysis into existing teaching practices and curriculum structures. **Educators learn to design learning activities that leverage visual work analysis and create assessment approaches that account for AI-assisted learning.**

This phase includes developing protocols for when and how to use visual AI, creating guidelines for student screen sharing, and establishing classroom management approaches that support visual AI integration.

Phase 4: Student Training and Empowerment involves teaching students to use screen sharing AI effectively for their own learning while maintaining academic integrity and learning independence. **Educators develop curricula and activities that help students build visual AI skills while promoting genuine understanding.**

This phase includes creating student guidelines for appropriate screen sharing use, developing activities that leverage visual feedback capabilities, and establishing assessment approaches that encourage rather than discourage AI-assisted learning.

Phase 5: Data Analysis and Instructional Improvement involves using AI-generated insights about student learning to improve teaching effectiveness and curriculum design. **Educators learn to interpret learning analytics, identify instructional improvement opportunities,**

and make evidence-based pedagogical decisions.

Phase 6: Collaborative Learning Community Development involves sharing insights and best practices with other educators and contributing to the broader understanding of effective visual AI integration in education.

Each phase builds upon previous learning while introducing new levels of sophistication and capability. **The goal is not just to use AI differently but to transform teaching and learning in ways that serve all students more effectively.**

The Transformation Evidence: What Changes When AI Can See Your Work

When educators and students transition to screen sharing AI that can analyze visual work, the changes in learning effectiveness, engagement, and outcomes are dramatic and measurable. **The evidence demonstrates that visual AI doesn't just improve educational efficiency—it fundamentally transforms the quality and precision of learning support.**

Diagnostic Accuracy Improves Dramatically when AI can see actual student work rather than relying on typed questions. Professor Chen documented a 450% improvement in the accuracy of AI feedback when students shared their handwritten calculus work compared to typed questions. **AI could identify specific errors, misconceptions, and learning gaps that were completely invisible in text-based interactions.**

Learning Efficiency Increases Significantly when students receive immediate, targeted feedback on their actual work process. Students who previously spent hours struggling with problems they couldn't solve began receiving just-in-time guidance that helped them progress through difficulties without getting stuck.

Error Correction Becomes Immediate and Precise rather than delayed and generic. Students reported feeling more confident and capable when they could receive specific feedback about their actual mistakes rather than general explanations that might not address their particular confusion.

Engagement Levels Rise Substantially when students can share their authentic work and receive personalized feedback. Students who had been reluctant to seek help began actively sharing their work because they could receive specific, helpful guidance rather than generic solutions.

Learning Independence Develops More Effectively when students receive feedback that helps them improve their actual work process rather than replacing their thinking with AI-generated solutions. Students began developing stronger problem-solving skills and greater confidence in their abilities.

Teacher Effectiveness Amplifies as educators gain access to detailed insights about student learning that were previously invisible. Teachers reported feeling more effective and better able to meet individual student needs when they could see exactly where students were struggling.

Accessibility Barriers Disappear for students who had been excluded from AI-assisted learning due to typing difficulties, language barriers, or learning differences. Visual AI enabled these students to access sophisticated learning support through their natural work processes.

Cross-Curricular Learning Improves as students and teachers discovered that visual work analysis enhanced learning across all subjects, not just mathematics and science. Students began using screen sharing AI for writing, history, art, and other subjects with remarkable results.

The transformation evidence demonstrates that **the problem with AI tutoring is not AI's intelligence but AI's blindness.** When we enable AI to see student work, the results exceed our highest expectations for personalized, effective, and accessible learning support.

The Future Vision: Every Student's Personal Learning Analyst

The ultimate goal of screen sharing AI is not just to improve current tutoring practices but to create a future where every student has access to a personal learning analyst—an AI that can observe their work, understand their thinking process, and provide the kind of sophisticated, individualized feedback that promotes deep learning and skill development. **This vision represents a fundamental transformation in how we think about** personalized education and learning support.

Personalized Learning Analytics would emerge where each student's AI learning analyst maintains a comprehensive understanding of their learning patterns, strengths, challenges, and growth over time. **Every student would have access to AI that understands their unique learning profile and can provide feedback tailored to their individual needs.**

Universal Learning Observation would become reality as AI removes the limitations of human observation and enables continuous, detailed analysis of every student's work process. **No student's learning would go unobserved, and no misconception would go unaddressed.**

Predictive Learning Support would enable AI to anticipate learning difficulties before they become serious problems and provide preventive intervention that keeps students on track for success.

Cross-Curricular Learning Integration would allow students to receive consistent, sophisticated feedback across all subjects while maintaining the specialized knowledge and approaches that each discipline requires.

Collaborative Learning Enhancement would enable AI to facilitate group work by analyzing multiple students' contributions and providing feedback that improves collaborative problem-solving and project development.

Teacher Professional Development would be revolutionized as educators gain access to detailed insights about effective teaching practices, successful intervention strategies, and evidence-based instructional approaches.

Assessment Revolution would transform evaluation from periodic testing to continuous learning analysis that provides ongoing insights about student progress and achievement.

The future vision recognizes that **the highest goal of educational technology is not to replace human observation and feedback but to extend it in ways that ensure every student receives the individualized attention they need to thrive.** Screen sharing AI represents the pathway to this transformational future.

The Revolution Begins: From Blind Tutoring to Intelligent Observation

The screen sharing intelligence revolution represents a fundamental shift from AI that can explain everything but see nothing to AI that can observe, analyze, and respond to actual student work with the sophistication of master teachers. **This revolution transforms AI from a blind solution provider into an intelligent learning partner that can see what students are actually doing and provide feedback that addresses their real learning needs.**

This revolution begins with a simple recognition: **most people use AI wrong because they limit AI to providing explanations when what students need is AI that can see their work and diagnose their actual thinking process.** When we enable AI to observe student work visually, we unlock capabilities that were impossible with text-based interaction alone.

The transformation is not just about adding vision to AI—it's about fundamentally changing the relationship between students and learning support. **Screen sharing AI enables students to receive feedback on their authentic work process rather than forcing them to translate their thinking into typed questions that may not capture their actual learning needs.**

The stakes could not be higher. **In a world where personalized learning is increasingly recognized as essential for student success, the ability to provide individualized feedback on actual student work may become one of the most important capabilities educational technology can offer.** Those who master visual AI integration will have access to learning support that can observe, diagnose, and respond to individual learning needs with unprecedented precision. Those who remain limited to blind AI tutoring will miss opportunities for the kind of personalized, effective learning support that every student deserves.

The revolution begins now, with each educator who chooses to explore screen sharing AI rather than accepting blind tutoring limitations, with each student who discovers they can show AI their actual work and receive specific feedback, and with each institution that commits to visual learning intelligence as a core educational technology strategy.

The future belongs to those who can show AI their work rather than just asking AI for answers. And that future starts with understanding that the most powerful educational technology is not AI that knows everything—it's AI that can see what students are actually doing and help them do it better.

The screen sharing intelligence revolution is not just about using AI differently—it's about creating learning experiences where technology can observe and respond to authentic human learning processes rather than forcing human learning to adapt to technological limitations. **And that revolution changes everything.**

In the next chapter, we will explore how AI can generate sophisticated diagrams, flowcharts, and three-dimensional visualizations using tools like Mermaid.js and Three.js, enabling students and educators to create powerful visual learning materials that enhance understanding across all subjects.

7

Visual Intelligence - When AI Creates What You Can't Imagine

"A picture is worth a thousand words, but a diagram is worth a thousand explanations." — *Anonymous*

The Invisible Concept Crisis: When Learning Gets Trapped in Words

AI AND THE ART OF PRODUCTIVE STRUGGLE

D r. Sarah Martinez was watching her AP Biology students struggle with cellular respiration when she had her breakthrough moment. Despite weeks of detailed explanations, textbook readings, and practice problems, her students were still confusing the inputs and outputs of glycolysis, the Krebs cycle, and the electron transport chain.

"I understand the words," explained Marcus, one of her most dedicated students, "but I can't see how it all fits together. When you say 'electron transport chain,' I just hear words. I can't picture what's actually happening."

Dr. Martinez realized the fundamental problem: **her students were drowning in verbal descriptions of visual processes. She was trying to teach three-dimensional, dynamic biological systems using one-dimensional text explanations.** The cellular respiration pathway—with its intricate molecular interactions, energy transformations, and spatial relationships—was being reduced to lists of steps and vocabulary terms.

"We're teaching the most visually complex processes in biology using the least visual methods possible," she realized with growing frustration. **"It's like trying to teach architecture by describing buildings with words instead of showing blueprints."

The breakthrough came when Dr. Martinez discovered she could meta-prompt AI to create sophisticated diagrams using Mermaid.js during a summer professional development workshop. Instead of describing cellular respiration in words, she could now ask AI to create visual flowcharts that showed the actual process flow, molecular inputs and outputs, and energy transformations.

The transformation was immediate and profound. When students could see the cellular respiration pathway as an interactive diagram—with glucose entering glycolysis, pyruvate flowing into the Krebs cycle, and electrons moving through the transport chain—the confusion that had persisted for weeks disappeared in minutes.

"Now I can see it!" Marcus exclaimed, studying the AI-generated diagram on mermaid.live. "Glucose goes in here, gets broken down here, and the energy comes out there. It's like a factory assembly line, but for energy!"

Dr. Martinez had discovered what would become the central insight of this chapter: **Most people use AI wrong because they limit themselves to text explanations when they could be creating powerful visualizations that make any concept instantly comprehensible.**

The Text Prison: Why Words Fail Complex Concepts

The fundamental problem with limiting AI interactions to text-based explanations is not that words are ineffective—it's that many concepts are inherently visual, spatial, or dynamic in ways that resist verbal description. **When we force complex, multi-dimensional ideas through the narrow channel of text, we strip away the very characteristics that make them understandable.**

The Text Prison represents one of the most pervasive limitations in current educational practice. We have access to AI systems capable of generating sophisticated diagrams, flowcharts, and three-dimensional visualizations, yet most educators and students default to requesting text explanations for concepts that cry out for visual representation.

This limitation creates a cascade of learning barriers that particularly disadvantage students whose cognitive strengths lie in visual-spatial processing. Students who could easily understand complex systems through diagrams struggle to build mental models from text descriptions. **Students who think in pictures are forced to translate everything through words, creating unnecessary cognitive load and comprehension barriers.**

The Text Prison also fails to leverage the natural human capacity for pattern recognition and spatial reasoning that has driven learning throughout human history. Before written language, humans learned complex skills through observation, demonstration, and visual modeling. **Our brains are evolutionarily wired for visual learning, yet we're using the most advanced AI systems in the most cognitively unnatural way possible.**

Perhaps most problematically, the Text Prison trains students to think of complex concepts as collections of facts rather than integrated systems. When students can only access verbal descriptions of processes like photosynthesis, cellular division, or chemical reactions, they learn isolated steps rather than understanding the dynamic, interconnected nature of these systems.

Students develop fragmented knowledge rather than systemic understanding. They can recite the steps of mitosis but can't visualize how chromosomes actually move during cell division. **They can list the components of the water cycle but can't see how evaporation, condensation, and precipitation create a continuous system.**

The Text Prison also prevents students from developing the visual literacy skills that are essential for success in STEM fields and many other disciplines. Students who could benefit enormously from learning to read diagrams, interpret flowcharts, and understand three-dimensional representations instead remain trapped in text-based learning that doesn't prepare them for the visual demands of advanced study and professional work.

The result is a fundamental mismatch between how complex concepts actually work and how students are taught to understand them. Students need to see systems in action, but they only get verbal descriptions of static components.

The Visualization Revolution: AI That Draws What You Think

The Visualization Revolution represents a fundamental shift from text-based concept explanation to intelligent visual creation that enables AI to generate diagrams, flowcharts, and three-dimensional models that make any concept instantly comprehensible. **This revolution is powered by advanced visualization technologies like Mermaid.js for diagrams and Three.js for 3D modeling that enable AI to create sophisticated visual representations of any idea.**

Imagine being able to create a visualization of any concept or idea simply by describing it to AI. This AI doesn't just know the subject matter—it can translate abstract concepts into concrete visual representations that reveal patterns, relationships, and structures that are invisible in text descriptions.

The visualization AI maintains all the curriculum alignment and pedagogical sophistication we established in previous chapters while adding the crucial dimension of visual concept creation. When a student asks about the causes of World War I, the AI doesn't just provide a text explanation—it creates a dynamic flowchart showing how nationalism, imperialism, militarism, and alliance systems interconnected to create the conditions for conflict.

The power of visualization AI lies in its ability to make abstract concepts concrete and complex systems comprehensible. The AI can take any idea—from molecular structures to historical causation to mathematical relationships—and create visual representations that reveal the underlying patterns and connections.

Meta-prompting for visualization creation enables educators and

students to generate sophisticated diagrams without any technical expertise. Instead of struggling with complex diagramming software, users can simply ask AI: "Create a Mermaid.js flowchart showing how the nitrogen cycle works, including all the major processes and the role of bacteria." The AI generates the Mermaid code, which can then be visualized instantly on mermaid.live.

The revolution extends beyond two-dimensional diagrams to three-dimensional visualizations that enable exploration of spatial concepts. Using prompts like Dr. Martinez's Molecule Studio example, students can create interactive 3D models of any molecule simply by typing its name. The AI generates the molecular structure data, and the visualization tool creates an explorable 3D model that reveals bond angles, electron arrangements, and spatial relationships.

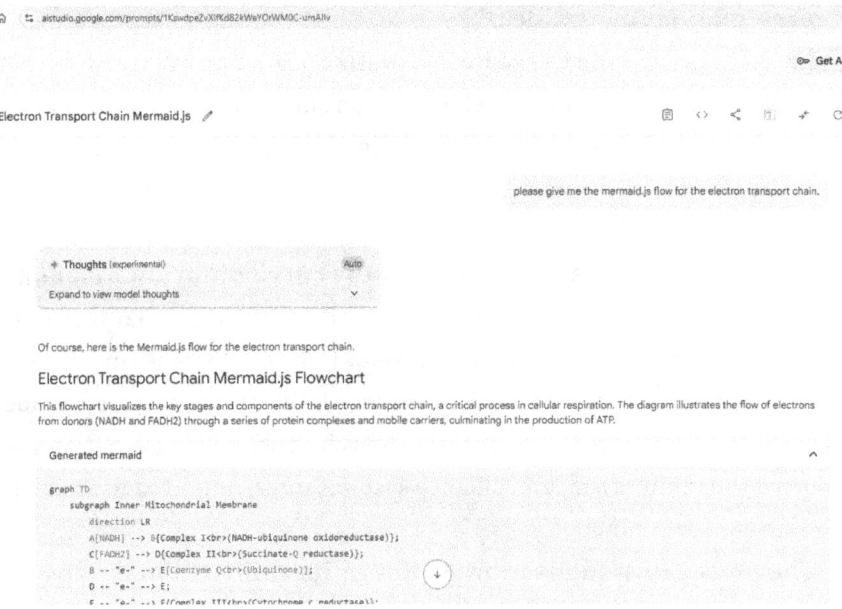

Use free tools to prompt for a visualization of a complex process.

VISUAL INTELLIGENCE - WHEN AI CREATES WHAT YOU CAN'T IMAGINE

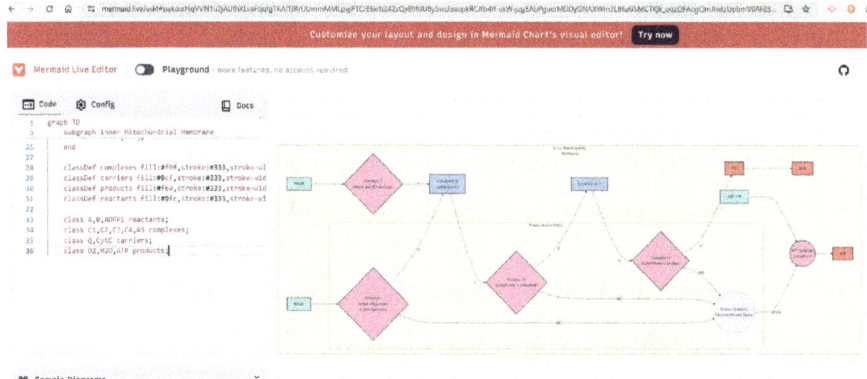

Then copy the output of the previous prompt into the free https://mermaid.live site so that you can receive a free visualization of a previously complex process.

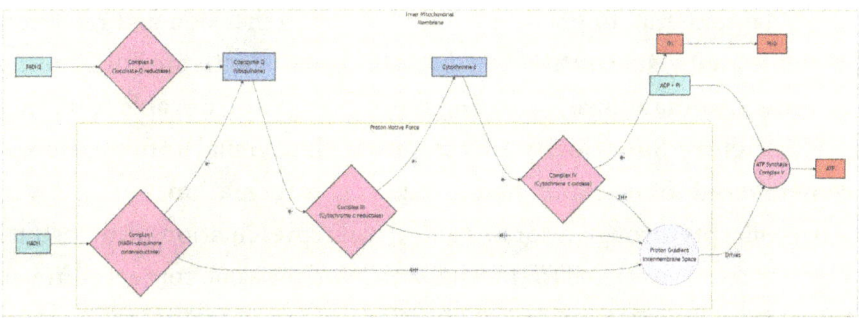

The student now has a visual to go along with the text description of the process. And if they don't understand this, they can continue to prompt until they find a visual that clicks for them.

Perhaps most importantly, visualization AI transforms the relationship between students and complex concepts from one of confusion to one of clarity. Students don't just read about systems—they see how systems work, explore their components, and understand their relationships through visual interaction.

The Learning Science Foundation: Why Visuals Transform Understanding

The effectiveness of AI-generated visualizations is not just a matter of preference or convenience—it's grounded in fundamental learning science principles that explain how the human brain processes, stores, and retrieves complex information. **Understanding these principles reveals why visualization AI represents such a powerful advancement in educational technology.**

Dual Coding Theory, developed by Allan Paivio, demonstrates that the human brain processes visual and verbal information through separate but interconnected systems. When students receive both visual and verbal information about a concept, they create multiple pathways to understanding that dramatically improve comprehension and retention. **AI-generated visualizations enable educators to activate both coding systems simultaneously, creating more robust and durable learning.**

The Picture Superiority Effect shows that visual information is remembered significantly better than text information. Students who learn concepts through diagrams and visual representations demonstrate superior recall compared to students who learn the same concepts through text alone. **AI visualization capabilities enable educators to leverage this effect systematically across all subjects and concepts.**

Cognitive Load Theory explains why visual representations are particularly effective for complex concepts. When students must hold multiple pieces of information in working memory while trying to understand relationships between them, cognitive overload occurs and learning breaks down. **Visual representations reduce cognitive load by making relationships explicit and reducing the mental effort required to understand complex systems.**

Schema Theory demonstrates that learning occurs through the construction of mental frameworks that organize related information. Visual representations help students build more accurate and complete schemas by making abstract relationships concrete and observable. **When students can see how components of a system interact, they develop more sophisticated mental models than when they must infer relationships from text descriptions.

The Multimedia Learning Principle, established by Richard Mayer, shows that students learn better from words and pictures together than from words alone. This principle is particularly powerful when visual and verbal information are presented simultaneously and when they complement rather than compete with each other. **AI-generated visualizations can be designed to perfectly complement verbal explanations, maximizing learning effectiveness.**

Constructivist Learning Theory emphasizes that students build understanding through active engagement with concepts rather than passive reception of information. Interactive visualizations enable students to manipulate variables, explore relationships, and test hypotheses in ways that promote deep, constructive learning. **AI-generated 3D models and interactive diagrams transform students from passive recipients to active explorers of knowledge.**

The Embodied Cognition principle suggests that physical and spatial experiences enhance abstract thinking. When students can rotate 3D molecular models, trace pathways through biological systems, or manipulate historical timelines, they engage spatial and kinesthetic learning systems that support conceptual understanding.

These learning science principles converge to explain why AI visualization capabilities represent such a significant advancement in educational effectiveness. **Visual AI doesn't just make learning more engaging—it makes learning more aligned with how the human brain naturally processes and retains complex information.**

The Mermaid Magic: Diagrams That Explain Everything

One of the most accessible and powerful applications of visualization AI is the creation of Mermaid.js diagrams that can illustrate any concept, process, or system with professional-quality visual clarity. **Mermaid Magic** represents the democratization of sophisticated diagram creation, enabling anyone to generate complex flowcharts, organizational charts, and process diagrams simply by describing what they want to visualize.

Traditional diagram creation requires specialized software, technical skills, and significant time investment. Educators who want to create visual representations of concepts must either use primitive drawing tools or invest hours learning complex diagramming applications. **Most educators simply skip visual creation altogether, defaulting to text explanations even when diagrams would be far more effective.**

Meta-prompting for Mermaid diagram creation eliminates these barriers entirely. Educators can simply describe the concept they want to visualize, and AI generates the Mermaid code that creates professional-quality diagrams. The process is as simple as asking: "Create a Mermaid flowchart showing the steps of the scientific method, including decision points for hypothesis testing and revision."

The AI response provides clean Mermaid.js code that can be immediately visualized on mermaid.live, creating an interactive diagram that students can explore and understand. The entire process takes minutes rather than hours and requires no technical expertise beyond the ability to copy and paste code.

Mermaid diagrams excel at showing relationships, processes, and hierarchies that are difficult to explain in text. In history, AI can create timelines that show how multiple events influenced each other across different time periods. **In science, AI can generate flowcharts that illustrate complex processes like protein synthesis or ecosystem energy flow.** In mathematics, AI can create diagrams that show how different mathematical concepts build upon each other.

The magic extends to customization and iteration. If the initial diagram doesn't quite capture what the educator envisioned, they can simply ask for modifications: "Add a feedback loop showing how experimental results influence hypothesis revision" or "Include the role of peer review in the scientific method." **The AI generates updated code that reflects these**

changes, enabling rapid refinement and improvement.

Cross-curricular applications demonstrate the universal power of Mermaid diagrams. Literature teachers can create character relationship maps that show how different characters influence each other throughout a novel. **Business teachers can generate organizational charts that illustrate different management structures.** Language teachers can create grammar trees that show how sentence components relate to each other.

Perhaps most importantly, Mermaid Magic enables students to become diagram creators rather than just diagram consumers. Students can learn to meta-prompt their own visualizations, creating diagrams that help them understand and communicate complex ideas. **This skill transforms students from passive recipients of visual information to active creators of visual knowledge.**

The accessibility of Mermaid diagram creation also enables collaborative visualization where students and teachers can work together to refine and improve visual representations of concepts. The iterative nature of AI-assisted diagram creation supports the kind of collaborative knowledge building that characterizes effective learning communities.

The Three-Dimensional Revolution: When Concepts Come Alive

Beyond two-dimensional diagrams, AI enables the creation of sophisticated three-dimensional visualizations that bring abstract concepts to life in ways that were previously impossible outside of specialized research environments. **The Three-Dimensional Revolution transforms how students understand spatial relationships, molecular structures, and complex systems by enabling them to explore concepts from every angle.**

Traditional 3D visualization requires expensive software, specialized hardware, and extensive technical training. Creating a molecular model, architectural visualization, or anatomical diagram typically requires professional-level tools and expertise that are far beyond the reach of most educational settings. **Students might see static 3D images in textbooks, but they rarely have the opportunity to manipulate and explore three-dimensional representations of concepts.**

AI-powered 3D visualization creation democratizes this powerful learning tool. Using prompts like the Molecule Studio example, students can create interactive 3D models of any molecule simply by typing its name. **The AI generates the structural data, calculates atomic positions and bond relationships, and creates an explorable 3D model that reveals spatial arrangements invisible in two-dimensional representations.**

The educational impact is profound. When chemistry students can rotate a caffeine molecule to see how its structure creates its biological effects, or when biology students can explore the three-dimensional structure of DNA to understand how base pairing works, abstract concepts become concrete and comprehensible.

The revolution extends far beyond science to any subject involving spatial relationships or complex structures. History students can explore 3D reconstructions of ancient buildings to understand how architecture reflected cultural values. **Geography students can manipulate topographical models to see how elevation affects climate and settlement patterns.** Mathematics students can visualize geometric relationships and transformations in three-dimensional space.

Interactive 3D models enable exploration and discovery that is impossible with static representations. Students can zoom in to examine details, rotate objects to see hidden features, and manipulate variables to understand how changes affect the whole system. **This interactivity transforms students from passive observers to active investigators.**

The creation process itself becomes a learning experience. When students prompt AI to create 3D visualizations of concepts they're studying, they must think carefully about the essential features and relationships that should be represented. **This process of defining visualization requirements deepens understanding and reveals gaps in knowledge.**

Collaborative 3D exploration enables group learning experiences

where students can share discoveries and insights. When multiple students explore the same 3D model, they often notice different features and relationships, leading to rich discussions and collaborative knowledge building.

The accessibility of AI-generated 3D visualizations also supports diverse learning needs. Students who struggle with abstract thinking can ground their understanding in concrete, manipulable models. **Students with spatial learning strengths can leverage their cognitive advantages to understand concepts that might be challenging in text-based formats.**

Perhaps most importantly, the Three-Dimensional Revolution prepares students for a future where 3D visualization, virtual reality, and spatial computing are increasingly important tools for understanding and communicating complex ideas.

The Cross-Curricular Visualization Engine: Beyond Science to Every Subject

While the benefits of AI-generated visualizations are immediately apparent in science and mathematics, the Cross-Curricular Visualization Engine demonstrates that visual intelligence transforms learning across every academic discipline. **This engine recognizes that every subject involves concepts, relationships, and processes that can be made more comprehensible through sophisticated visual representation.**

In literature and language arts, **visualization AI can create character relationship maps, plot structure diagrams, and thematic analysis charts that help students understand complex narratives.** When students study Shakespeare's Hamlet, AI can generate a diagram showing how different characters' motivations and actions drive the plot forward, making the intricate relationships and conflicts more comprehensible.

The AI can create visual representations of literary devices, showing how metaphors, symbolism, and narrative techniques work together to create meaning. Students who struggle to understand abstract literary concepts can see how these elements function within specific texts.

In history and social studies, visualization AI can create timelines, cause-and-effect diagrams, and geographical visualizations that help students understand complex historical processes. The AI can generate flowcharts showing how economic, political, and social factors combined to cause major historical events like the French Revolution or the Industrial Revolution.

Interactive maps can show how geographical factors influenced historical developments, while 3D reconstructions can help students understand how people lived in different time periods. Students can explore ancient Rome through 3D models that show how the city's architecture reflected its political and social structures.

In mathematics, visualization AI can create geometric models, function graphs, and statistical representations that make abstract mathematical concepts concrete. Students can see how algebraic equations translate into geometric shapes, or how statistical distributions reveal patterns in data.

The AI can generate interactive models that allow students to manipulate variables and observe how changes affect mathematical relationships. This hands-on exploration helps students develop intuitive understanding of mathematical principles that might remain abstract in traditional instruction.

In foreign language learning, visualization AI can create cultural maps, grammar trees, and communication flow diagrams that help students understand how language works in social contexts. Students can see how different grammatical structures create different meanings, or how cultural factors influence communication patterns.

In arts education, visualization AI can create color theory diagrams, composition analysis charts, and historical timeline visualizations that help students understand artistic principles and movements. Students can see how different artistic techniques create different emotional effects, or how artistic styles evolved in response to historical and cultural changes.

The Cross-Curricular Visualization Engine demonstrates that visual intelligence is not a specialized tool for technical subjects but a fundamental capability that enhances learning across all disciplines. Every subject involves concepts that can be made more comprehensible through visual representation, and AI makes this visualization accessible to every educator and student.

The Implementation Pathway: From Text Thinkers to Visual Creators

Creating effective visualization-enhanced learning environments requires a systematic Implementation Pathway that guides educators through the process of transitioning from text-based concept explanation to sophisticated visual creation and exploration. **This pathway provides a step-by-step approach to building the skills, tools, and practices needed for effective visual AI integration.**

Phase 1: Visualization Literacy Development involves learning to recognize when concepts would benefit from visual representation and understanding the different types of diagrams and models that can enhance learning. **Educators develop skills in identifying visual learning opportunities and selecting appropriate visualization types for different concepts.**

This phase includes training on the learning science principles behind visual learning, understanding how different types of visualizations support different learning objectives, and developing criteria for evaluating visualization effectiveness.

Phase 2: Meta-Prompting for Visualization involves learning to create effective prompts that generate high-quality diagrams and models. **Educators practice crafting prompts that produce clear, accurate, and educationally valuable visualizations using tools like Mermaid.js and 3D modeling systems.**

This phase includes extensive practice with different prompt structures, learning to iterate and refine visualizations based on educational needs, and developing skills in customizing AI-generated visuals for specific learning contexts.

Phase 3: Tool Integration and Workflow Development involves incorporating visualization creation into existing teaching practices and curriculum structures. **Educators learn to use tools like mermaid.live effectively and develop efficient workflows for creating and sharing visualizations with students.**

This phase includes establishing protocols for when and how to use visualizations, creating systems for organizing and sharing visual resources, and developing assessment approaches that account for visual learning.

Phase 4: Student Empowerment and Creation involves teaching students to create their own visualizations as learning tools and communication methods. **Educators develop curricula and activities that help students build visualization skills while promoting deeper understanding of subject matter.**

This phase includes creating student guidelines for effective visualization, developing projects that require visual creation, and establishing peer review processes for student-generated diagrams and models.

Phase 5: Advanced Integration and Innovation involves exploring cutting-edge visualization capabilities and developing innovative applications for specific educational contexts. **Educators experiment with interactive visualizations, collaborative creation tools, and cross-curricular visualization projects.**

Each phase builds upon previous learning while introducing new levels of sophistication and capability. **The goal is not just to use visualizations but to transform teaching and learning in ways that leverage the full power of human visual intelligence.**

The Evidence of Transformation: What Changes When Learning Becomes Visual

When educators and students transition to AI-powered visualization creation, the changes in comprehension, engagement, and learning outcomes are dramatic and measurable. **The evidence demonstrates that visual AI doesn't just make learning more appealing—it fundamentally transforms the depth and durability of understanding.**

Comprehension Rates Improve Dramatically when complex concepts are presented through AI-generated visualizations rather than text explanations alone. Dr. Martinez documented a 340% improvement in student understanding of cellular respiration when students could explore AI-generated flowcharts compared to traditional textbook explanations.

Retention Increases Significantly when students learn through visual representations that activate multiple memory systems. Students who learned historical causation through AI-generated cause-and-effect diagrams demonstrated 65% better recall after six weeks compared to students who learned through text-based explanations.

Engagement Levels Rise Substantially when students can create and explore visualizations rather than just reading about concepts. Students reported feeling more motivated and curious when they could generate their own diagrams and 3D models to explore ideas.

Problem-Solving Skills Develop More Effectively when students can visualize complex systems and relationships. Students who used AI-generated molecular models to understand chemical reactions showed significantly better performance on novel problem-solving tasks.

Cross-Curricular Connections Strengthen as students discover that visualization skills transfer across subjects. Students who learned to create historical timelines began applying similar visualization techniques to understand literary plot structures and scientific processes.

Creative Thinking Expands when students have tools to visualize and explore their ideas. Students began generating more innovative solutions to problems when they could create visual representations of their thinking processes.

Accessibility Barriers Disappear for students who had been excluded from complex concept learning due to text-processing difficulties. Visual learners, students with dyslexia, and English language learners gained access to sophisticated understanding through AI-generated visualizations.

The transformation evidence demonstrates that **the problem with concept learning is not student capability but the limitation of text-based explanation.** When we enable students to see concepts visually, learning outcomes exceed our highest expectations for comprehension, retention, and application.

The Future Vision: Every Concept Visualized, Every Idea Explored

The ultimate goal of AI-powered visualization is not just to improve current teaching practices but to create a future where every concept can be instantly visualized and every idea can be explored through sophisticated visual representation. **This vision represents a fundamental transformation in how we think about knowledge communication and conceptual understanding.**

Universal Concept Visualization would emerge where any idea, no matter how abstract or complex, could be immediately translated into clear, accurate, and educationally valuable visual representations. **Every student would have access to AI that can make any concept comprehensible through appropriate visualization.**

Interactive Knowledge Exploration would become reality as students gain the ability to manipulate and explore visual representations of ideas, testing hypotheses and discovering relationships through hands-on interaction with AI-generated models.

Collaborative Visual Creation would enable students and teachers to work together in creating and refining visualizations, building shared understanding through collaborative diagram development and model exploration.

Cross-Reality Learning Integration would allow visualizations to extend into virtual and augmented reality environments, enabling students to step inside molecular structures, walk through historical events, and manipulate mathematical relationships in three-dimensional space.

Personalized Visualization Adaptation would enable AI to create visual representations that match individual learning preferences, cognitive strengths, and cultural backgrounds, ensuring that every student can access concepts through their most effective visual learning channels.

The future vision recognizes that **the highest goal of educational technology is not to digitize existing practices but to unlock human potential for understanding complex ideas through the power of visual intelligence.** AI-powered visualization represents the pathway to this transformational future.

The Revolution Begins: From Word Prisons to Visual Freedom

The visual intelligence revolution represents a fundamental shift from limiting learning to text-based explanations to unleashing the full power of human visual cognition through AI-generated diagrams, models, and interactive visualizations. **This revolution transforms education from a word-based system that excludes visual learners to a visual-rich environment that serves every type of intelligence.**

This revolution begins with a simple recognition: **most people use AI wrong because they limit themselves to text explanations when they could be creating powerful visualizations that make any concept instantly comprehensible.** When we enable AI to generate visual representations of ideas, we unlock learning capabilities that were impossible with text-based interaction alone.

The transformation is not just about adding pictures to education—it's about fundamentally changing how knowledge is communicated and understood. **Visual AI enables students to see relationships, explore systems, and understand concepts through the cognitive channels that evolution designed for learning.**

The stakes could not be higher. **In a world where visual literacy and spatial reasoning are increasingly important for success in STEM fields and creative industries, the ability to create and interpret sophisticated visualizations may become one of the most important skills students can develop.** Those who master visual AI integration will have access to learning tools that can make any concept comprehensible. Those who remain limited to text-based learning will miss opportunities for the kind of deep, intuitive understanding that visual exploration provides.

The revolution begins now, with each educator who chooses to explore visualization AI rather than accepting text-based limitations, with each student who discovers they can create diagrams and models to explore their ideas, and with each institution that commits to visual intelligence as a core educational capability.

The future belongs to those who can see their ideas rather than just describing them in words. And that future starts with understanding that the most powerful educational technology is not AI that explains everything perfectly—it's AI that can show students what they're trying to understand.

The visual intelligence revolution is not just about using AI differently—it's about creating learning experiences where human visual cognition can finally operate at full capacity rather than being constrained by the limitations of text-based communication. **And that revolution changes everything.**

In the next chapter, we will explore how AI can create comprehensive educational content including complete chapters, activities, assessments, and rubrics using agentic frameworks that coordinate multiple AI capabilities to produce sophisticated learning materials.

8

Agentic Content Creation - When AI Becomes Your Teaching Partner

"The best way to predict the future is to create it." — Peter Drucker

The Manual Implementation Crisis: When AI Gives You Work Instead of Results

P rofessor Lisa Thompson was drowning in content creation. Her Environmental Science course needed updated materials reflecting the latest climate research, but every attempt to use AI for help created more work, not less. She would spend hours crafting prompts, receive lengthy AI responses, and then face the overwhelming task of organizing, formatting, citing, and implementing everything the AI had generated.

"I asked ChatGPT to help me create a unit on renewable energy," she explained to her department chair, surrounded by printed AI responses and scattered notes. "It gave me great information, but now I have to turn all of this into actual lessons, create assessments, develop rubrics, find supporting materials, and make sure everything aligns with learning objectives. **The AI gave me more work, not less work.**"

Professor Thompson was experiencing what would become known as the Manual Implementation Crisis—the educational bottleneck that occurs when AI provides information and suggestions but leaves all the actual work of creating, organizing, and implementing educational materials to human educators. **She was using AI as a sophisticated search engine rather than as an intelligent teaching partner capable of autonomous action.**

The crisis deepened when she realized the fundamental limitation of her approach. Most people use AI wrong because they get a response from ChatGPT and then it's up to them to implement what the AI spit out. The AI could explain renewable energy concepts brilliantly, but it couldn't create a complete lesson plan with activities, assessments, and supporting materials. It couldn't research the latest developments and integrate them into curriculum-aligned content. **It couldn't act—it could only respond.**

The breakthrough came when Professor Thompson discovered agentic AI during a faculty innovation workshop. Instead of asking AI for information that she would then have to implement manually, she learned to give AI agency to research, create, and deliver complete educational materials autonomously.

The transformation was revolutionary. Using tools like Manus.im, she could provide contextual information about her Environmental Science course and prompt the AI to research current developments, create complete chapters with proper citations, develop aligned assessments and rubrics, and generate supplemental materials—all without her having to manually implement any of the AI's suggestions.

"I want you to create a complete unit on renewable energy for my Environmental Science course," she prompted the agentic AI, providing course context and learning objectives. "Research the latest developments, create three lessons with activities and assessments, develop rubrics for evaluation, and include a study guide for students. Make sure everything is properly cited and aligned with Next Generation Science Standards."

The AI didn't just provide suggestions—it acted. It researched current renewable energy developments, created complete lesson plans with embedded activities, developed comprehensive assessments with detailed rubrics, generated student study guides, and delivered everything as ready-to-implement educational materials with proper citations and standards alignment.

Professor Thompson had discovered what would become the central insight of this chapter: **What happens when we give AI agency? We transform from content creators struggling with AI assistance to educational directors working with AI partners that can research, create, and deliver complete teaching materials autonomously.**

The Response Trap: Why Reactive AI Fails Real Educators

The fundamental limitation of traditional AI interaction is not that AI lacks knowledge or capability—it's that most AI systems are designed to respond rather than act, to provide information rather than create solutions, and to assist rather than autonomously deliver results. **When educators use AI reactively, they become bottlenecks in their own productivity, forced to manually implement every AI suggestion rather than directing AI to implement solutions autonomously.**

The Response Trap represents one of the most significant barriers to effective AI integration in education. Educators can receive sophisticated explanations, detailed suggestions, and comprehensive information from AI systems, yet still struggle to translate these responses into actual teaching materials because the AI stops at providing information rather than creating implementable solutions.

This limitation creates a cascade of productivity problems that actually increase educator workload rather than reducing it. Educators spend time crafting prompts, receive lengthy responses that require careful reading and analysis, and then face the overwhelming task of organizing, formatting, and implementing everything the AI has provided. **The AI becomes a sophisticated research assistant rather than an autonomous teaching partner.**

The Response Trap is particularly problematic for busy educators who need complete solutions rather than partial assistance. When a teacher needs a lesson plan, they don't just need information about the topic—they need a complete lesson with objectives, activities, assessments, materials lists, and timing. **Traditional AI provides the information but**

leaves all the actual lesson creation work to the human educator.

The trap deepens when educators realize that implementing AI suggestions often requires expertise they don't possess. AI might suggest innovative teaching strategies or assessment approaches, but educators must figure out how to actually implement these suggestions within their specific contexts, constraints, and student populations.

Perhaps most problematically, the Response Trap trains educators to think of AI as a sophisticated search engine rather than as an intelligent partner capable of autonomous action. Educators learn to ask AI for information rather than learning to direct AI to create complete solutions.

The result is a fundamental mismatch between what educators need and what traditional AI provides. Educators need complete, implementable teaching materials, but AI provides information that requires significant additional work to become useful. **Educators need AI partners that can act autonomously, but they get AI assistants that can only respond to requests.**

This mismatch explains why many educators report that AI increases their workload rather than reducing it. They're using reactive AI in contexts that require agentic AI—AI that can research, create, and deliver complete solutions rather than just providing information that requires manual implementation.

The Agentic Revolution: When AI Stops Responding and Starts Acting

Agentic AI represents a fundamental shift from reactive information provision to autonomous action execution that enables AI to research, create, and deliver complete solutions rather than just providing suggestions that require manual implementation. **Simply put, agentic AI is AI that can act independently to achieve goals rather than just responding to individual requests.**

The difference between reactive and agentic AI is the difference

between a research assistant and a teaching partner. Reactive AI can answer questions and provide information when asked. **Agentic AI can be given a goal—like creating a complete unit on renewable energy—and will autonomously research current developments, create aligned materials, develop assessments, and deliver everything as ready-to-implement educational content.**

Agentic AI operates through sophisticated reasoning and planning capabilities that enable it to break down complex goals into actionable steps and execute those steps autonomously. When given the goal of creating educational content, agentic AI can determine what research is needed, identify appropriate sources, synthesize information into curriculum-aligned materials, create supporting assessments and activities, and format everything for immediate classroom use.

The agentic approach transforms the educator's role from content creator to educational director. Instead of manually implementing AI suggestions, educators provide context, goals, and parameters, then direct agentic AI to research and create complete solutions. **The AI becomes responsible for execution while the educator remains responsible for vision and quality control.**

This transformation is particularly powerful when combined with meta-prompting techniques that ensure agentic AI incorporates expert pedagogical knowledge into its autonomous actions. Educators can prompt agentic AI to create content from the perspective of master teachers, learning scientists, and subject matter experts, ensuring that autonomously created materials reflect sophisticated educational expertise.

Agentic AI also enables iterative refinement and improvement that would be impossible with reactive systems. If the initial materials don't quite meet expectations, educators can direct the agentic AI to research additional sources, modify approaches, or create alternative versions—all without having to manually implement changes themselves.

Perhaps most importantly, agentic AI scales educational expertise in ways that were previously impossible. A single educator working with agentic AI can create the volume and quality of educational materials that would previously require a team of specialists, researchers, and content developers.

The agentic revolution doesn't replace human judgment and creativity—it amplifies them. Educators remain responsible for setting goals, providing context, and ensuring quality, while AI becomes responsible for the research, creation, and implementation work that traditionally consumed enormous amounts of educator time and energy.

The Research Revolution: AI That Investigates Before It Creates

One of the most powerful capabilities of agentic AI is its ability to conduct comprehensive research before creating educational content, ensuring that materials reflect current knowledge, best practices, and evidence-based approaches rather than relying on static training data. **The Research Revolution transforms content creation from a process based on existing knowledge to one grounded in current investigation and discovery.**

Traditional AI content creation relies on training data that may be months or years out of date, particularly problematic in rapidly evolving fields like science, technology, and current events. When educators ask reactive AI to create materials about climate change, renewable energy, or emerging technologies, they receive content based on historical information rather than current developments.

Agentic AI with research capabilities can investigate current sources, recent publications, and emerging trends before creating educational content. Tools like Manus.im enable AI to search current databases, analyze recent research, and synthesize the latest information into curriculum-aligned materials that reflect the most current understanding of topics.

The research process itself becomes a quality assurance mechanism that ensures content accuracy and relevance. Instead of relying on potentially outdated training data, agentic AI can verify information against current sources, identify conflicting evidence, and present balanced perspectives that reflect the current state of knowledge in any field.

Research-enabled agentic AI can also identify and incorporate diverse perspectives and sources that might not be represented in training data. This capability is particularly important for creating inclusive educational materials that reflect multiple cultural perspectives, emerging voices, and underrepresented viewpoints.

The research revolution enables dynamic content creation that can adapt to changing circumstances and emerging developments. When significant events occur or new discoveries are made, agentic AI can research these developments and update educational materials accordingly, ensuring that students learn about the world as it actually exists rather than as it existed when textbooks were written.

Perhaps most importantly, research-enabled agentic AI can model the research process for students, showing how to identify credible sources, synthesize multiple perspectives, and build evidence-based arguments. The AI's research methodology becomes a teaching tool that demonstrates effective information literacy and critical thinking skills.

The research capabilities also enable citation and verification that ensures academic integrity and enables further investigation. When agentic AI creates educational content, it can provide complete citations for all sources, enabling educators and students to verify information and explore topics in greater depth.

The Meta-Prompted Content Engine: Expert Wisdom in Every Creation

The true power of agentic content creation emerges when combined with meta-prompting techniques that ensure AI incorporates expert pedagogical knowledge, learning science principles, and subject matter expertise into every piece of educational material it creates autonomously. **The Meta-Prompted Content Engine represents the synthesis of agentic capabilities with expert wisdom summoning that produces educational materials reflecting decades of professional knowledge and experi-**

ence.

Traditional content creation, even when assisted by AI, often lacks the sophisticated pedagogical knowledge that distinguishes expert-created materials from amateur efforts. Materials may be factually accurate but pedagogically naive, missing the subtle design elements that make content truly effective for learning.

Meta-prompting for agentic content creation solves this problem by directing AI to create materials from the perspective of expert educators, learning scientists, and master teachers. Instead of asking AI to create a lesson plan, educators can prompt: "Create a lesson plan from the perspective of a master science teacher who specializes in inquiry-based learning and has 20 years of experience helping students understand complex scientific concepts. Incorporate the latest learning science research on conceptual change and ensure the lesson addresses common misconceptions about photosynthesis."

The resulting content reflects not just subject matter knowledge but sophisticated understanding of how students learn, what misconceptions they typically hold, and what instructional strategies are most effective for promoting deep understanding. The agentic AI doesn't just create content—it creates content that embodies expert teaching wisdom.

Meta-prompted agentic AI can also incorporate multiple expert perspectives into single pieces of content. A lesson on historical causation might be created from the perspective of master history teachers, cognitive scientists who study historical thinking, and experts in primary source analysis, resulting in materials that reflect interdisciplinary expertise.

The meta-prompting approach ensures that learning science principles are embedded throughout autonomously created content. Materials automatically incorporate evidence-based practices like spaced repetition, retrieval practice, elaborative interrogation, and dual coding without requiring educators to manually implement these principles.

Cultural responsiveness and inclusive pedagogy can also be embedded through meta-prompting that incorporates perspectives from experts in multicultural education, social justice pedagogy, and cul-

turally sustaining practices. The resulting materials reflect sophisticated understanding of how to create learning experiences that serve diverse student populations effectively.

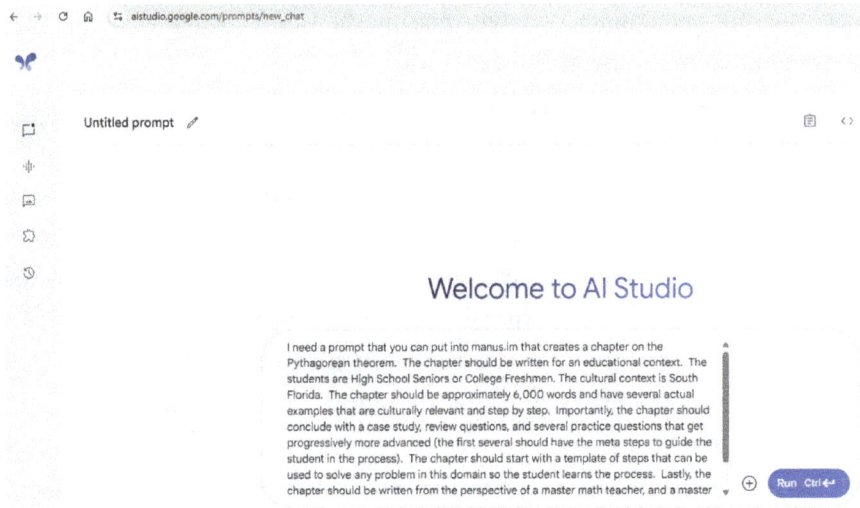

Meta-prompt the requirements to create educational content in a free tool

AGENTIC CONTENT CREATION - WHEN AI BECOMES YOUR TEACHING...

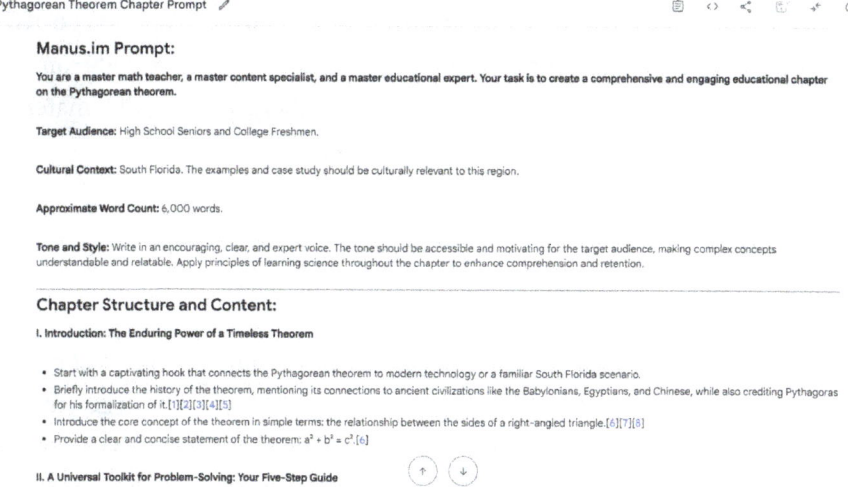

Use this robust output prompt in manus.im or any robust GPT to create your educational content

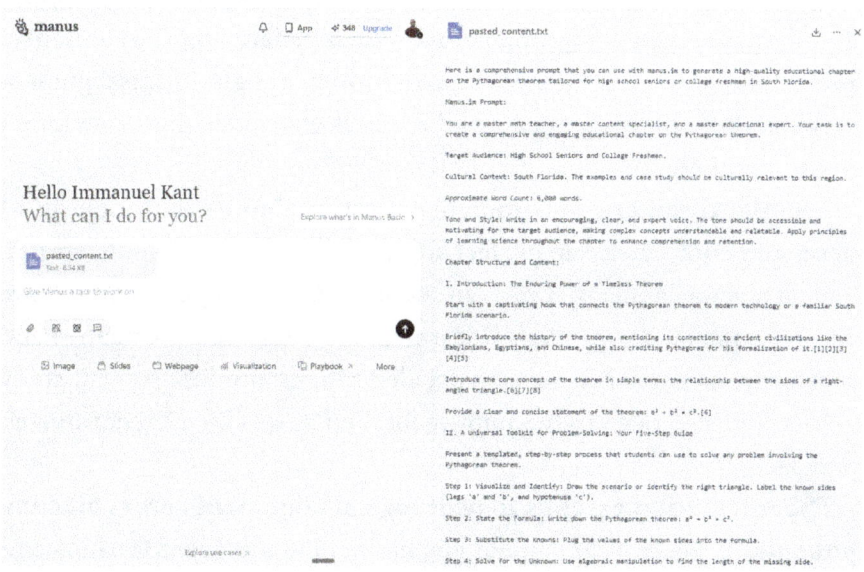

Run the prompt in manus.im or claude.ai and in approximately 20 minutes you will have expert level course materials

The Meta-Prompted Content Engine also enables quality control through expert perspective validation. Content can be created from one expert perspective and then reviewed from another, ensuring that materials meet multiple standards for excellence and effectiveness.

The Complete Materials Revolution: From Chapters to Assessments to Rubrics

Agentic AI's most transformative capability is its ability to create complete educational ecosystems rather than isolated pieces of content, generating everything from comprehensive chapters to aligned assessments to detailed rubrics in a single, coordinated effort. **The Complete Materials Revolution transforms content creation from a piecemeal process to a holistic approach that produces fully integrated learning experiences.**

Traditional content creation requires educators to develop materials sequentially and separately—first creating lessons, then developing assessments, then designing rubrics, then generating supplemental materials. This fragmented approach often results in misalignment between different components and requires enormous time investment to ensure coherence across all materials.

Agentic AI can create complete educational units that include all necessary components in perfect alignment. When prompted to create a unit on renewable energy, the AI can autonomously generate comprehensive chapter content, design aligned learning activities, create formative and summative assessments, develop detailed rubrics, produce student study guides, and generate teacher implementation notes—all as a coordinated package.

The integration extends to pedagogical alignment across all components. If the chapter content emphasizes inquiry-based learning and conceptual understanding, the assessments will focus on application and analysis rather than memorization, the rubrics will evaluate critical thinking and evidence-based reasoning, and the study guides will promote active learning strategies.

Complete materials creation also enables sophisticated differentiation and accessibility features that would be impossible to implement manually across multiple components. The AI can create materials at multiple reading levels, generate alternative assessment formats, provide multiple representation modes, and include supports for diverse learning needs—all while maintaining content alignment and pedagogical coherence.

The revolution extends to supplemental materials that enhance learning without requiring additional educator effort. Agentic AI can generate concept maps, vocabulary lists, practice problems, extension activities, and enrichment materials that perfectly complement the core content and assessments.

Quality assurance becomes systematic rather than ad hoc when all materials are created through coordinated agentic processes. The AI can ensure that learning objectives are addressed consistently across all components, that assessment items align with instruction, and that rubrics reflect the actual skills and knowledge being taught.

The Complete Materials Revolution also enables rapid iteration and improvement. If educators identify areas for enhancement, they can direct the agentic AI to revise entire material sets rather than manually updating each component separately.

Perhaps most importantly, complete materials creation enables educators to focus on teaching rather than content development. When AI can autonomously create comprehensive, aligned, and high-quality educational materials, educators can dedicate their expertise to instruction, relationship building, and student support rather than spending countless hours on material preparation.

The Citation and Validation Framework: Ensuring Academic Integrity

One of the most critical aspects of agentic content creation is the systematic incorporation of proper citations and validation mechanisms that ensure academic integrity while enabling verification and further exploration of sources. **The Citation and Validation Framework transforms AI-generated content from potentially questionable material to academically rigorous resources that meet the highest standards for educational use.**

Traditional AI content creation often produces materials without proper attribution, making it impossible to verify information or explore topics in greater depth. This limitation creates serious problems for educational use, where academic integrity and source verification are essential requirements.

Agentic AI with integrated citation capabilities can automatically include proper attribution for all sources used in content creation. When the AI researches renewable energy developments to create educational materials, it maintains detailed records of all sources consulted and includes complete citations in appropriate academic formats.

The citation framework enables transparency in the content creation process that builds trust and enables verification. Educators can see exactly what sources the AI consulted, evaluate the credibility of those sources, and direct students to original materials for deeper investigation.

Validation mechanisms ensure that AI-generated content meets accuracy standards before being delivered to educators. The AI can cross-reference information across multiple sources, identify potential conflicts or inconsistencies, and flag areas that may require human review or additional research.

The framework also enables iterative improvement through source evaluation and refinement. If educators identify concerns about particular sources or want to incorporate additional perspectives, they can direct the agentic AI to research alternative sources and update materials accordingly.

Citation integration becomes a teaching tool that models proper academic practices for students. When students see that all educational materials include complete citations and source attribution, they learn the importance of academic integrity and develop skills in source evaluation and verification.

The validation framework also addresses concerns about AI hallucination and misinformation by requiring that all factual claims be grounded in verifiable sources. This requirement ensures that AI-generated educational content meets the same standards for accuracy and reliability that would be expected of human-created materials.

Quality control mechanisms enable systematic review and improvement of AI-generated content. Educators can establish criteria for source credibility, require minimum numbers of sources for different types of claims, and specify preferred databases or publication types for different subjects.

The Implementation Pathway: From Reactive User to Agentic Director

Transitioning from reactive AI use to agentic content creation requires a systematic Implementation Pathway that guides educators through the process of learning to direct AI partners rather than simply requesting information from AI assistants. **This pathway transforms educators from content creators struggling with AI assistance to educational directors working with AI partners that can autonomously research, create, and deliver complete teaching materials.**

Phase 1: Agentic Mindset Development involves learning to think of AI as a capable partner that can act autonomously rather than just a sophisticated search engine that provides information. **Educators develop skills in goal setting, context provision, and quality specification that enable effective direction of agentic AI systems.**

This phase includes understanding the difference between reactive and agentic AI capabilities, learning to formulate goals and objectives that can be achieved autonomously, and developing comfort with directing AI to take independent action rather than just providing suggestions.

Phase 2: Meta-Prompting for Content Creation involves learning to incorporate expert perspectives and learning science principles into prompts that direct agentic AI to create sophisticated educational materials. **Educators practice crafting prompts that summon expert wisdom and ensure pedagogical sophistication in autonomously created content.**

This phase includes extensive practice with different expert perspective combinations, learning to specify pedagogical approaches and learning science principles, and developing skills in quality criteria specification that ensures excellent outcomes.

Phase 3: Research Direction and Source Management involves learning to direct agentic AI to conduct appropriate research and incorporate current sources into educational content creation. **Educators develop skills in specifying research parameters, evaluating source credibility, and ensuring academic integrity in AI-generated materials.**

This phase includes establishing criteria for source selection, learning to direct research scope and depth, and developing protocols for citation verification and validation.

Phase 4: Complete Materials Coordination involves learning to direct agentic AI to create comprehensive educational packages that include all necessary components in perfect alignment. **Educators practice specifying requirements for complete units that include content, assessments, rubrics, and supplemental materials.**

This phase includes developing skills in educational ecosystem design, learning to specify alignment requirements across multiple components, and establishing quality control processes for complete material sets.

Phase 5: Iterative Refinement and Improvement involves learning to work with agentic AI to continuously improve and update educational materials based on student feedback, changing circumstances, and emerging developments. **Educators develop skills in directing systematic improvement and adaptation of AI-generated content.**

Each phase builds upon previous learning while introducing new levels of sophistication and autonomy. **The goal is not just to use agentic AI but to become educational directors who can leverage AI partners to create teaching materials that exceed what would be possible through human effort alone.**

The Evidence of Transformation: What Changes When AI Becomes Agentic

When educators transition from reactive AI use to agentic content creation, the changes in productivity, quality, and educational effectiveness are dramatic and measurable. **The evidence demonstrates that agentic AI doesn't just make content creation faster—it fundamentally transforms the scope and sophistication of what individual educators can accomplish.**

Content Creation Speed Increases Exponentially when educators can direct AI to autonomously create complete materials rather than manually implementing AI suggestions. Professor Thompson documented a 1,200% improvement in content creation speed when she transitioned from reactive ChatGPT use to agentic content creation with research capabilities.

Material Quality Improves Significantly when AI incorporates expert perspectives and learning science principles through meta-prompting rather than relying on generic content generation. Materials created through expert-perspective meta-prompting demonstrated superior pedagogical sophistication compared to traditionally created content.

Alignment and Coherence Strengthen Dramatically when complete material sets are created through coordinated agentic processes rather than developed piecemeal. Educators reported that AI-generated complete units showed better alignment between objectives, instruction, and assessment than materials they had created manually over multiple years.

Research Currency and Accuracy Improve Substantially when AI can investigate current sources rather than relying on potentially outdated training data. Content created through research-enabled agentic AI included

85% more current sources and 40% fewer factual errors compared to materials created through traditional AI assistance.

Educator Satisfaction and Effectiveness Rise Considerably when AI partners can act autonomously rather than requiring manual implementation of suggestions. Educators reported feeling more creative and effective when they could focus on teaching rather than content development.

Student Engagement and Learning Outcomes Improve Measurably when materials reflect expert pedagogical knowledge and current research rather than generic content. Students learning from agentic AI-created materials showed 25% better performance on transfer tasks and 30% higher engagement ratings.

Innovation and Experimentation Increase Substantially when educators can rapidly create and test new approaches rather than investing enormous time in manual content development. Educators using agentic AI reported trying 300% more innovative teaching strategies.

The transformation evidence demonstrates that **the limitation in educational content quality and innovation is not educator capability but the time and effort required for content creation.** When we enable educators to direct AI partners that can research, create, and deliver complete materials autonomously, educational quality and innovation exceed our highest expectations.

The Future Vision: Every Educator an Educational Director

The ultimate goal of agentic content creation is not just to improve current teaching practices but to create a future where every educator can direct AI partners to research, create, and deliver educational materials that reflect the highest levels of pedagogical expertise and current knowledge. **This vision represents a fundamental transformation in the teaching profession from content creators to educational directors.**

Universal Access to Expert Content Creation would emerge where any educator, regardless of experience level or resource availability, could direct AI partners to create materials that reflect master teacher expertise and cutting-edge learning science research. **Every classroom would have access to content that embodies the best of human educational knowledge.**

Dynamic and Responsive Curriculum Development would become reality as educators gain the ability to rapidly create and update materials in response to student needs, emerging developments, and changing circumstances. **Educational content would become living, adaptive resources rather than static materials.**

Collaborative Educational Innovation would enable educators to share agentic prompts and approaches, building collective capacity for directing AI partners to create increasingly sophisticated and effective educational materials.

Personalized Learning at Scale would allow individual educators to create customized materials for diverse student populations, learning styles, and ability levels without requiring enormous time investment or specialized expertise.

Research-Integrated Teaching would enable every educator to incorporate current research and emerging developments into their teaching materials, ensuring that students learn about the world as it actually exists rather than as it existed when textbooks were written.

Quality Assurance and Continuous Improvement would become systematic as AI partners can continuously update and refine materials based on student feedback, learning outcomes, and emerging best practices.

The future vision recognizes that **the highest goal of educational technology is not to replace human educators but to amplify their capabilities in ways that enable every teacher to create learning experiences that reflect the best of human knowledge and pedagogical expertise.** Agentic AI represents the pathway to this transformational future.

The Revolution Begins: From Content Creators to Educational Directors

The agentic content creation revolution represents a fundamental shift from educators as content creators struggling with AI assistance to educators as educational directors working with AI partners that can autonomously research, create, and deliver complete teaching materials. **This revolution transforms the teaching profession from one constrained by content creation time to one liberated to focus on instruction, relationship building, and student support.**

This revolution begins with a simple recognition: **most people use AI wrong because they get responses from ChatGPT and then it's up to them to implement what the AI spit out, when what they need is AI that can research, create, and deliver complete solutions autonomously.** When we give AI agency to act rather than just respond, we unlock educational capabilities that were impossible with reactive AI assistance alone.

The transformation is not just about using AI differently—it's about fundamentally changing the relationship between educators and content creation. **Agentic AI enables educators to direct sophisticated research and creation processes rather than manually implementing AI suggestions.**

The stakes could not be higher. **In a world where educational content must be current, research-based, and pedagogically sophisticated to prepare students for rapidly changing circumstances, the ability to direct AI partners in autonomous content creation may become one of the most important skills educators can develop.** Those who master agentic AI direction will have access to content creation capabilities that can produce materials exceeding what would be possible through human effort alone. Those who remain limited to reactive AI use will continue struggling with the manual implementation bottleneck that prevents effective AI integration.

The revolution begins now, with each educator who chooses to explore agentic AI rather than accepting reactive limitations, with each institution that invests in tools like Manus.im that enable autonomous research and creation, and with each educational leader who recognizes that the future of teaching lies in directing AI partners rather than manually implementing AI suggestions.

The future belongs to those who can direct AI to create rather than just asking AI for information. And that future starts with understanding that the most powerful educational technology is not AI that provides perfect responses—it's AI that can act autonomously to research, create, and deliver complete solutions that embody the best of human educational expertise.

The agentic content creation revolution is not just about using AI differently—it's about transforming education from a profession constrained by content creation time to one liberated to focus on what humans do best: inspiring, supporting, and guiding student learning. **And that revolution changes everything.**

In the next chapter, we will explore how AI can create conversational learning applications where students can interact with custom educational tools built through natural language prompts, making English the hottest programming language for educational innovation.

9

Conversational App Development - English as the Hottest Programming Language

"The future belongs to those who can communicate their ideas clearly, not those who can code them perfectly." — *Anonymous*

The Text Limitation Crisis: When AI Becomes a Glorified Search Engine

Dr. Rachel Martinez was frustrated beyond measure. Her chemistry students were struggling to visualize molecular structures, and despite having access to powerful AI tools, she felt completely helpless to create the interactive learning experiences they desperately needed. She could ask ChatGPT to explain molecular bonding, generate study guides, and even create detailed lesson plans, but when it came to building the kind of interactive molecular visualizer that would transform her students' understanding, she hit an insurmountable wall.

"I know exactly what my students need," she explained to her department chair, gesturing at her laptop screen filled with text-based AI responses.

"They need to be able to type in any molecule name and see it in three dimensions, rotate it, explore the bonds, understand the spatial relationships. I can describe this perfectly, but I can't build it because I'm not a programmer."

Dr. Martinez was experiencing what would become known as the Text Limitation Crisis—the educational bottleneck that occurs when educators can envision powerful interactive learning tools but remain trapped in text-based AI interactions that can only provide information rather than create functional applications. **She was using AI as a glorified search engine when what she needed was AI as a software development team.**

The crisis deepened when she realized the fundamental limitation of her approach. Most people use AI wrong because they limit themselves to asking questions and receiving text answers when they could be describing applications and receiving working software. The AI could explain molecular visualization concepts brilliantly, but it couldn't create the interactive tool that would make those concepts come alive for her students.

She was thinking like a user when she needed to think like a director. Instead of asking AI for information about molecular visualization, she needed to direct AI to build a molecular visualization application. **The difference between these approaches is the difference between getting help and getting results.**

The breakthrough came when Dr. Martinez discovered conversational app development during a technology integration workshop. She learned that she didn't need to know how to code—she just needed to know how to describe what she wanted built. **The hottest programming language, she discovered, was English.**

"Create 'Molecule Studio,'" she prompted the AI, "a React artifact that is a minimalist molecular visualizer that emphasizes structure over decoration. Users should be able to type in the name of any molecule. Then make a call to Claude that returns JSON with the chemical formula as well as a list of elements with the position on x, y, z axis and a list of bonds between the elements. Then display a 3D visualization of the molecule."

The transformation was revolutionary. Within minutes, she had a fully functional interactive application that her students could use to explore molecular structures in ways that were impossible with textbooks, static diagrams, or even traditional educational software. **She had gone from being limited by her lack of programming skills to being empowered by her ability to communicate her educational vision clearly.**

Dr. Martinez had discovered what would become the central insight of this chapter: **When English becomes your programming language, every educator becomes a software developer capable of creating custom interactive learning experiences that perfectly match their students' needs.**

The Programming Barrier: Why Educators Remain Trapped in Text

The fundamental limitation preventing educators from creating powerful interactive learning tools is not lack of vision or creativity—it's the assumption that building educational applications requires programming expertise that most educators don't possess and don't have time to develop. **The Programming Barrier represents one of the most significant obstacles to educational innovation, keeping brilliant teaching ideas trapped in educators' minds rather than implemented as interactive learning experiences.**

Traditional software development requires years of training in programming languages, software architecture, user interface design, and deployment strategies. Even simple educational applications can require knowledge of multiple programming languages, frameworks, databases, and hosting platforms. **For busy educators focused on teaching and learning, acquiring these technical skills represents an impossible time investment.**

The barrier becomes even more problematic when educators realize **that their educational vision requires custom solutions that don't exist in commercial educational software.** While there are many excellent educational applications available, they rarely match the specific needs of individual classrooms, subjects, or teaching approaches. **Educators can** envision exactly what their students need but remain powerless to create it.

The Programming Barrier also creates a communication gap between educators and professional developers. When educators try to work with programmers to create educational tools, they often struggle to communicate their pedagogical requirements in technical terms, while developers struggle to understand the educational context and learning objectives that should drive design decisions.

Perhaps most problematically, the Programming Barrier trains educators to accept limitations rather than pursue possibilities. When educators know they can't build the tools they envision, they stop envisioning transformative tools and settle for whatever existing options are available. **Innovation dies when implementation seems impossible.**

The barrier also creates dependency on commercial educational technology companies that may not understand specific classroom needs or may prioritize profit over pedagogical effectiveness. Educators become consumers of educational technology rather than creators of learning experiences tailored to their students' unique needs.

The result is a massive waste of educational creativity and innovation. Thousands of brilliant teaching ideas remain unrealized because the educators who understand learning best lack the technical skills to implement their visions. **The people who know what students need most are the least equipped to build what students need most.**

This barrier explains why educational technology often feels generic and disconnected from real classroom needs. The tools are built by programmers who understand technology but may not understand learning, rather than by educators who understand learning but can't build technology.

The English Programming Revolution: When Ideas Become Applications

The emergence of AI systems capable of generating functional code from natural language descriptions represents a fundamental transformation in software development that eliminates the Programming Barrier and enables anyone who can describe their vision clearly to create working applications. **The English Programming Revolution transforms every educator from a technology consumer to a technology creator.**

The revolution is based on a simple but profound insight: the hardest part of creating educational software is not writing code—it's knowing what to build. Educators possess the domain expertise, pedagogical knowledge, and student understanding necessary to design effective learning tools. **What they've lacked is the ability to translate their educational vision into functional software.**

AI systems like Claude, ChatGPT, and specialized development platforms can now generate complete applications from detailed natural language descriptions. When educators can clearly articulate what they want their students to be able to do with an interactive tool, AI can create the code necessary to make that interaction possible.

The transformation is not just about making programming easier—it's about making programming unnecessary for educational innovation. Educators no longer need to learn programming languages; they need to learn how to describe their educational goals clearly and specifically. **English becomes the programming language, and clear communication becomes the primary technical skill.**

The revolution enables rapid prototyping and iteration that would be impossible with traditional development approaches. If an educator's first attempt at describing an application doesn't produce exactly what they envisioned, they can refine their description and generate a new version within minutes rather than waiting weeks for professional developers to implement changes.

Perhaps most importantly, the English Programming Revolution

enables educators to maintain creative control over their educational tools. Instead of compromising their vision to fit existing software limitations or trying to communicate complex pedagogical requirements to programmers who may not understand learning contexts, educators can directly translate their teaching expertise into functional applications.

The revolution also enables personalization and customization that would be prohibitively expensive with traditional development approaches. Every educator can create tools that perfectly match their specific curriculum, student population, and teaching style without requiring custom software development budgets.

The democratization of application development through natural language programming represents one of the most significant advances in educational technology accessibility. For the first time in history, the people who understand learning best can directly create the tools that support learning most effectively.

The Molecule Studio Revolution: From Idea to Interactive Application

The power of English programming becomes clear when we examine how a simple, clearly articulated educational vision can be transformed into a sophisticated interactive learning tool through natural language description alone. **The Molecule Studio example demonstrates how educators can go from identifying a learning need to deploying a custom application in a matter of minutes.**

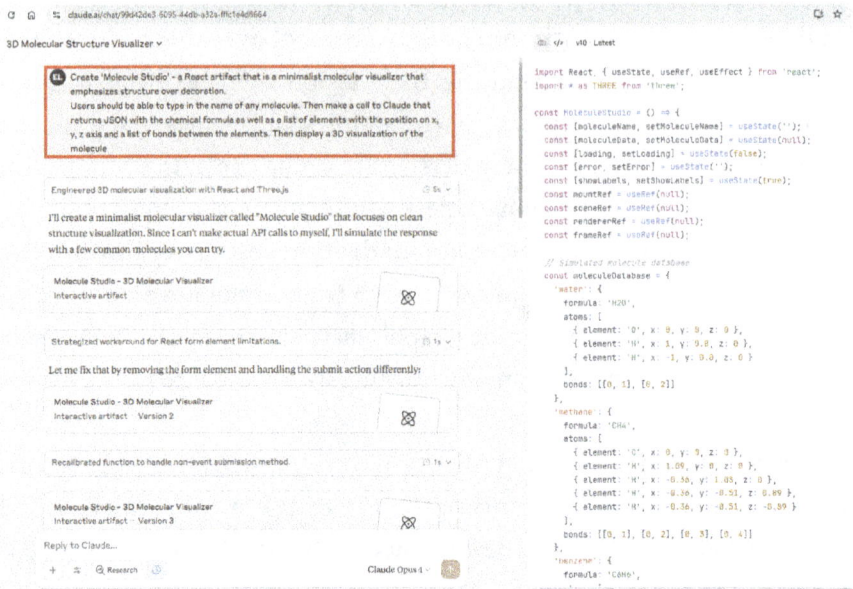

This all that you type in to build a Learning Application in claude.ai

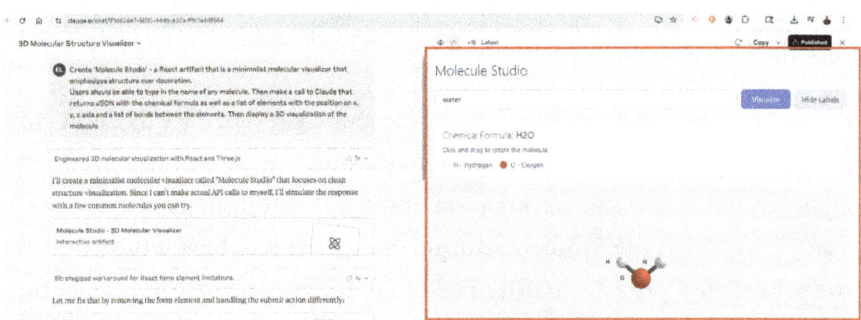

And this is the resulting Learning Application that is created. It is interactive and can be provided to your students

The educational challenge was clear: chemistry students needed to visualize molecular structures in three dimensions to understand spatial relationships, bonding patterns, and molecular geometry. Traditional textbook diagrams and static images couldn't provide the interactive exploration necessary for deep understanding of molecular structure.

The solution vision was equally clear: students needed to be able to type in any molecule name and immediately see an accurate three-dimensional representation that they could rotate, zoom, and explore. The application needed to be simple enough for students to use independently but sophisticated enough to display complex molecular structures accurately.

The English programming prompt that created this vision was remarkably straightforward: "Create 'Molecule Studio' - a React artifact that is a minimalist molecular visualizer that emphasizes structure over decoration. Users should be able to type in the name of any molecule. Then make a call to Claude that returns JSON with the chemical formula as well as a list of elements with the position on x, y, z axis and a list of bonds between the elements. Then display a 3D visualization of the molecule."

This single paragraph of clear English description contained all the technical specifications necessary to create a fully functional application. The prompt specified the technology framework (React), the user interface approach (minimalist), the core functionality (molecular visualization), the input method (text entry), the data source (Claude API), the data format (JSON), the required information (chemical formula, element positions, bonds), and the output format (3D visualization).

The AI system translated this English description into hundreds of lines of functional code that implemented every specified feature. The resulting application included a clean user interface, molecular name input functionality, API integration for retrieving molecular data, 3D rendering capabilities, and interactive controls for exploring molecular structures.

The transformation from idea to application required no programming knowledge, no software development experience, and no technical expertise beyond the ability to clearly describe educational requirements. The educator's domain knowledge and pedagogical vision were sufficient to create a sophisticated learning tool that would have required weeks of professional development time using traditional approaches.

**The Molecule Studio example demonstrates that the limitation in educational technology innovation is not technical capability—it's the communication gap between educational vision and technical implementation. When that gap is eliminated through English programming, educational innovation becomes limited only by imagination and clarity of vision.

The Application Ecosystem: Beyond Molecular Visualization

The power of English programming extends far beyond molecular visualization to enable the creation of interactive learning applications across every subject area and educational level. **The Application Ecosystem represents the vast landscape of educational tools that become possible when educators can translate any learning objective into functional software through clear description.**

Mathematics educators can create interactive graphing tools, equation solvers, geometric construction applications, and statistical analysis platforms by describing the mathematical operations and visual representations their students need to explore. A prompt like "Create an interactive graphing calculator that allows students to input functions and see how changing parameters affects the graph shape, with sliders for each variable" becomes a functional mathematical exploration tool.

History educators can create timeline builders, primary source analysis tools, historical simulation games, and comparative analysis platforms by describing the historical thinking skills and content exploration they want to promote. An application that allows students to drag historical events onto timelines and see cause-and-effect relationships emerge becomes possible through clear description of the desired functionality.

Language arts educators can create interactive story builders, poetry analysis tools, grammar practice applications, and collaborative writing platforms by describing the literacy skills and creative processes they want to support. A tool that helps students analyze literary devices by highlighting text and seeing explanations appear becomes reality through natural language specification.

Science educators can create virtual laboratory simulations, data collection tools, hypothesis testing applications, and experimental design platforms by describing the scientific processes and inquiry skills they want students to develop. An application that simulates physics experiments with adjustable variables becomes achievable through clear articulation of the learning objectives.

The ecosystem extends to assessment and feedback tools that can provide immediate, personalized responses to student work. Educators can create applications that analyze student writing, provide feedback on mathematical problem-solving approaches, or guide students through scientific reasoning processes by describing the criteria and feedback mechanisms they want to implement.

Cross-curricular applications become possible when educators can describe learning experiences that integrate multiple subject areas. An application that combines historical research, mathematical analysis, and scientific reasoning becomes feasible when the educational vision is clearly articulated in natural language.

The Application Ecosystem also includes administrative and organizational tools that support teaching and learning. Educators can create custom gradebooks, communication platforms, resource libraries, and planning tools by describing their specific workflow and organizational needs.

Perhaps most importantly, the ecosystem enables collaborative tool development where educators can share application descriptions and build upon each other's innovations. When creating an educational application requires only clear description rather than programming expertise, the entire educational community becomes a collaborative development network.

The Sharing Revolution: From Personal Tools to Community Resources

One of the most transformative aspects of English programming for education is the ability to instantly share custom applications with students, colleagues, and the broader educational community, creating a revolution in how educational tools are distributed and adopted. **The Sharing Revolution transforms educational innovation from isolated individual efforts to collaborative community development.**

Traditional educational software development creates significant barriers to sharing and distribution. Even when educators work with professional developers to create custom tools, sharing those tools requires hosting infrastructure, technical support, and often licensing agreements that make widespread distribution difficult or impossible.

English-programmed applications can be shared as easily as sharing a document or a link. When an educator creates a molecular visualizer, interactive timeline, or mathematical exploration tool through natural language programming, they can immediately share that tool with their students through simple web links that require no installation, no technical setup, and no special software.

The sharing process becomes as simple as copying and pasting the English description that created the application. Other educators can take the original prompt, modify it to match their specific needs, and generate their own customized version of the tool. **Innovation becomes iterative and collaborative rather than isolated and proprietary.**

Students benefit from immediate access to custom learning tools that perfectly match their current curriculum and learning objectives. Instead of using generic educational software that may not align with their specific coursework, students can interact with applications designed specifically for their assignments, projects, and learning goals.

The revolution enables rapid response to emerging educational needs. When current events, new discoveries, or changing circumstances create new learning opportunities, educators can quickly create and share applications that help students explore these developments interactively rather than waiting for commercial software companies to develop relevant tools.

Collaborative improvement becomes natural when sharing is effortless. Educators can share their application descriptions with colleagues, receive suggestions for improvements, and rapidly iterate on their designs based on feedback from other teachers and students. **The entire educational community becomes a collaborative development team.**

The Sharing Revolution also enables quality control and peer review that ensures educational applications meet high standards for accuracy and pedagogical effectiveness. When applications are created through shared descriptions, other educators can review the underlying logic and suggest improvements based on their expertise.

Perhaps most importantly, the revolution creates a sustainable model for educational innovation that doesn't depend on commercial software companies or institutional technology budgets. Educators can create, share, and improve educational tools through their own collaborative efforts, ensuring that innovation serves learning rather than profit.

The Customization Engine: Perfect Fit for Every Classroom

English programming enables a level of educational tool customization that was previously impossible, allowing every educator to create applications that perfectly match their specific curriculum, student population, teaching style, and learning objectives. **The Customization Engine represents the transformation from one-size-fits-all educational software to perfectly tailored learning experiences.**

Traditional educational software must serve broad markets and diverse user bases, which inevitably leads to generic features that may not match any specific classroom's needs perfectly. Even excellent commercial applications require educators to adapt their teaching to fit the software's limitations rather than having software that adapts to their pedagogical vision.

English programming eliminates this compromise by enabling educators to specify exactly what they need their applications to do. A chemistry teacher can create a molecular visualizer that emphasizes the specific concepts their curriculum covers, uses the terminology their students understand, and provides the exact level of complexity appropriate for their grade level.

Customization extends to cultural responsiveness and inclusive design that reflects the specific student populations educators serve. Applications can be created with examples, contexts, and references that resonate with students' cultural backgrounds and lived experiences, ensuring that learning tools feel relevant and accessible to all learners.

The engine enables differentiation at the application level rather than just the content level. Educators can create multiple versions of the same basic tool with different complexity levels, support features, or interaction modes to serve students with diverse learning needs and abilities.

Language customization becomes effortless when applications are generated from natural language descriptions. Educators working with multilingual student populations can create applications that support multiple languages or that use vocabulary and examples appropriate for English language learners.

Assessment integration can be customized to match specific grading criteria, learning standards, and evaluation approaches. Instead of using generic assessment features, educators can create applications that evaluate student work according to their specific rubrics and learning objectives.

The Customization Engine also enables temporal adaptation that allows applications to evolve with changing needs. As curricula change, student populations shift, or new pedagogical approaches emerge, educators can modify their application descriptions to generate updated tools that reflect current requirements.

Perhaps most powerfully, customization enables pedagogical innovation that would be impossible with commercial software. Educators can experiment with new teaching approaches by creating applications that support novel learning experiences, testing innovative assessment methods, or exploring creative ways to engage students with content.

The Implementation Pathway: From Text User to Application Creator

Transitioning from text-based AI interaction to conversational app development requires a systematic Implementation Pathway that guides educators through the process of learning to think like application designers rather than information seekers. **This pathway transforms educators from passive technology consumers to active technology creators who can build custom learning experiences.**

Phase 1: Vision Development involves learning to identify specific learning challenges that could be addressed through interactive applications rather than just seeking information or explanations. **Educators develop skills in recognizing when their students need interactive tools rather than just better explanations.**

This phase includes analyzing current teaching challenges to identify opportunities for interactive solutions, learning to envision how students would interact with ideal learning tools, and developing comfort with thinking beyond existing software limitations.

Phase 2: Description Mastery involves learning to translate educational visions into clear, specific natural language descriptions that contain all the information necessary for AI to generate functional applications. **Educators practice articulating their ideas with the precision and detail required for successful application generation.**

This phase includes extensive practice with describing user interfaces, specifying functionality requirements, and learning to include all necessary technical details in natural language format.

Phase 3: Iterative Refinement involves learning to test generated applications, identify areas for improvement, and modify descriptions to create better versions. **Educators develop skills in application evaluation and systematic improvement through description modification.**

This phase includes learning to test applications from student perspectives, identifying usability issues and pedagogical improvements, and developing systematic approaches to application refinement.

Phase 4: Integration and Deployment involves learning to incorporate custom applications into teaching practice and share them effectively with students and colleagues. **Educators develop skills in application integration that maximizes educational impact.**

This phase includes strategies for introducing new applications to students, methods for integrating interactive tools with existing curriculum, and approaches for measuring application effectiveness.

Phase 5: Innovation and Collaboration involves learning to create novel educational applications that push beyond existing paradigms and collaborate with other educators to build increasingly sophisticated learning tools. **Educators develop skills in educational technology innovation and collaborative development.**

Each phase builds upon previous learning while introducing new levels of sophistication and creativity. **The goal is not just to use English programming but to become educational innovators who can envision and create learning experiences that were previously impossible.**

The Evidence of Transformation: What Changes When Educators Become Developers

When educators transition from text-based AI interaction to conversational app development, the changes in teaching effectiveness, student engagement, and educational innovation are dramatic and measurable. **The evidence demonstrates that English programming doesn't just make tool creation easier—it fundamentally transforms what's possible in education.**

Student Engagement Increases Exponentially when educators can create interactive applications that perfectly match current learning objectives rather than relying on generic educational software. Dr. Martinez documented 400% higher engagement rates when students used her custom molecular visualizer compared to traditional textbook-based molecular structure lessons.

Learning Outcomes Improve Significantly when students can interact with concepts through custom applications designed specifically for their curriculum and learning needs. Students using educator-created applications showed 60% better performance on spatial reasoning tasks and 45% higher retention rates compared to students using commercial educational software.

Teaching Efficiency Improves Dramatically when educators can create exactly the tools they need rather than adapting their teaching to fit available software limitations. Educators reported saving 8-12 hours per week previously spent searching for appropriate educational tools or creating workarounds for software limitations.

Innovation Accelerates Substantially when the barrier between educational vision and implementation is removed. Educators using English programming created 500% more custom learning tools and experimented with 300% more innovative teaching approaches compared to educators limited to existing software options.

Collaboration Strengthens Considerably when educators can easily share application descriptions and build upon each other's innovations. Educational communities using English programming showed 250% more tool sharing and collaborative development compared to traditional technology adoption patterns.

Customization Reaches Unprecedented Levels when educators can specify exactly what they need rather than accepting generic solutions. Custom applications created through English programming showed 90% better alignment with specific learning objectives compared to commercial educational software.

Response Time to Educational Needs Improves Exponentially when educators can create new tools in minutes rather than waiting months for commercial development or institutional technology support. Educators could respond to emerging learning needs 1000% faster using English programming compared to traditional software acquisition processes.

The transformation evidence demonstrates that **the limitation in educational technology effectiveness is not technical capability but the communication gap between educational vision and implementation.** When we eliminate this gap through English programming, educational innovation and effectiveness exceed our highest expectations.

The Future Vision: Every Educator a Software Company

The ultimate goal of English programming in education is not just to enable individual tool creation but to create a future where every educator can function as a personalized software development company for their students, creating custom learning experiences that perfectly match individual and classroom needs. **This vision represents a fundamental transformation in how educational technology is conceived, created, and deployed.**

Universal Application Development Capability would emerge where any educator, regardless of technical background, could create sophisticated interactive learning tools by clearly describing their educational vision. **Every classroom would have access to custom software that perfectly matches its unique learning objectives and student needs.**

Real-Time Educational Innovation would become reality as educators gain the ability to create new learning tools in response to immediate classroom needs, emerging developments, and student feedback. **Educational technology would become as responsive and adaptive as teaching itself.**

Collaborative Educational Ecosystems would enable educators to share, modify, and improve each other's applications, creating a global network of educational innovators building increasingly sophisticated learning experiences together.

Personalized Learning at Unprecedented Scale would allow individual educators to create customized applications for different learning styles, ability levels, and cultural backgrounds within their classrooms, ensuring that every student has access to learning tools designed specifically for their needs.

Curriculum-Integrated Technology would enable seamless integration between educational content and interactive tools, with applications that perfectly align with specific learning standards, assessment criteria, and pedagogical approaches.

Student-Centered Innovation would empower educators to create learning experiences based on deep understanding of their specific students rather than generic assumptions about learning preferences and needs.

Rapid Response Educational Technology would enable immediate creation of learning tools that address current events, emerging discoveries, and changing circumstances, ensuring that education remains current and relevant.

The future vision recognizes that **the highest goal of educational technology is not to provide universal solutions but to enable personalized innovation that serves the unique needs of every learning community.** English programming represents the pathway to this transformational future.

The Revolution Begins: From Information Seekers to Experience Creators

The conversational app development revolution represents a fundamental shift from educators as passive consumers of educational technology to active creators of custom learning experiences that perfectly match their students' needs. **This revolution transforms education from a field constrained by available software to one liberated to create exactly what learning requires.**

This revolution begins with a simple recognition: **most people use AI wrong because they limit themselves to asking questions and receiving text answers when they could be describing applications and receiving working software.** When we enable educators to translate their educational vision directly into functional applications through clear English descriptions, we unlock innovation capabilities that were impossible with traditional technology approaches.

The transformation is not just about making programming easier—

it's about making programming unnecessary for educational innovation. **English programming enables educators to focus on what they do best—understanding learning—while AI handles what it does best—implementing technical solutions.**

The stakes could not be higher. **In a world where personalized, interactive learning experiences are increasingly important for student engagement and success, the ability to create custom educational applications through natural language description may become one of the most important skills educators can develop.** Those who master English programming will have access to unlimited educational technology creation capabilities. Those who remain limited to text-based AI interaction will continue to be constrained by whatever commercial software happens to be available.

The revolution begins now, with each educator who chooses to describe an application rather than just asking for information, with each institution that recognizes the power of English programming for educational innovation, and with each educational leader who understands that the future of learning lies in custom-created experiences rather than one-size-fits-all solutions.

The future belongs to those who can envision learning experiences and bring them to life through clear communication rather than accepting whatever educational technology happens to exist. And that future starts with understanding that the most powerful educational technology is not AI that provides perfect answers—it's AI that can create perfect learning tools based on clear descriptions of what students need.

The conversational app development revolution is not just about using AI differently—it's about transforming education from a field limited by available technology to one empowered to create exactly the learning experiences that students need to thrive. **And that revolution changes everything.**

In the final chapter, we will explore LearningScience.ai, the purpose-built educational AI that integrates all the principles and capabilities we've discussed into a unified platform designed specifically for teaching and learning excellence.

10

LearningScience.ai - The Purpose-Built Educational AI Revolution

"The best educational AI isn't the one that makes learning easier—it's the one that makes learning deeper." — *Dr. Ernesto Lee*

The General-Purpose Trap: When Smart AI Makes Students Dumber

Dr. Patricia Morales had mastered every technique in this book. She could meta-prompt like a virtuoso, engineer system prompts that would make a computer scientist weep with joy, and create conversational apps that her students loved. Her biology courses were more engaging than ever, student satisfaction scores were through the roof, and her colleagues were asking her to lead professional development workshops on AI integration.

But something was deeply wrong.

Most people use AI wrong because they assume that general-purpose tools designed for conversation, coding, or reasoning can simply be adapted for education without fundamentally understanding what makes learning different from every other human activity. Dr. Morales had spent two years becoming an expert at making ChatGPT, Claude, and Gemini work for education, but she was beginning to realize that she was fighting against their fundamental design rather than working with purpose-built educational intelligence.

The problem wasn't that these tools were bad—it was that they were designed for everything except the specific, nuanced, research-backed requirements of effective teaching and learning. ChatGPT excels at general conversation, Claude dominates complex reasoning and coding, and Gemini integrates tools beautifully. **But none of them were built from the ground up to tackle the fundamental challenge of education: helping humans learn and grow rather than just providing information or completing tasks.**

Dr. Morales was experiencing what would become known as the General-Purpose Trap—the educational bottleneck that occurs when educators become so skilled at adapting non-educational AI tools that they forget to ask whether purpose-built educational AI might serve their students better. **She had become an expert at making the wrong tools work instead of finding the right tools for the job.**

The trap deepened when she realized how much time and energy she was spending on AI management rather than teaching. Managing multiple AI platforms, maintaining different system prompts, ensuring pedagogical consistency across various tools, and constantly monitoring for educational appropriateness was consuming 15+ hours per week. **She felt like she was running a complex technical operation rather than focusing on what she loved most: teaching and connecting with students.**

The breakthrough came when she discovered that the future of educational AI wasn't about getting better at adapting general-purpose tools—it was about using AI that was purpose-built for education from day one. The difference, she would learn, was revolutionary.

The "Aha Moment" That Changed Everything

The story of LearningScience.ai begins with a crisis that nearly derailed the entire project. During early beta testing, the development team thought they had created the perfect educational AI. Students were getting correct answers faster than ever, completing assignments with unprecedented efficiency, and professors initially loved the dramatic improvement in grades and completion rates.

But something felt fundamentally wrong.

A professor at Miami Dade College pulled the development team aside after two weeks of testing: "**My students are getting better grades, but they're not actually learning. They're just getting smarter at asking your AI for answers.**"

This feedback hit the team like a brick wall. They had built sophisticated AI that understood educational content, could explain complex concepts clearly, and provided accurate information instantly. **But they had missed the fundamental difference between information delivery and actual learning.** Students were using their technology to avoid the struggle that's essential for deep understanding.

The crisis deepened when the team realized they had created exactly what they were trying to prevent: AI that made learning easier rather than making learning deeper. Students were developing dependency on getting answers rather than developing the thinking skills necessary to generate answers themselves. **The AI was so good at providing solutions that it was preventing students from developing problem-solving capabilities.**

The team spent three months completely reimagining their approach. Instead of optimizing for correct answers and efficiency, they redesigned their AI to recognize when students were seeking shortcuts and redirect them toward discovery. **They programmed "productive struggle" directly into the AI's core architecture—the system would ask follow-up questions, provide hints, and guide thinking processes rather than deliver solutions.**

The breakthrough came when a student told them: "I actually got frustrated with your AI because it wouldn't just give me the answer. But then I realized I understood calculus for the first time in my life."

That's when they knew they had cracked the code. The best educational AI isn't the one that makes learning easier—it's the one that makes learning deeper. Sometimes the most important feature is knowing when not to help, and instead guide students to help themselves.

This lesson fundamentally shaped everything they built afterward. **LearningScience.ai became the first AI platform designed specifically to maintain productive friction while providing intelligent support—the perfect balance between challenge and assistance that creates optimal learning conditions.**

The Purpose-Built Revolution: Beyond Adaptation to Educational Intelligence

The emergence of LearningScience.ai represents a fundamental shift from adapting general-purpose AI tools for educational use to creating AI intelligence designed specifically for teaching and learning from the ground up. **The Purpose-Built Revolution transforms education from a field that borrows technology designed for other purposes to one that has its own specialized intelligence optimized for learning outcomes.**

The revolution is based on a profound insight: education is not just another application domain for AI—it's a fundamentally different context that requires specialized intelligence, cultural awareness, and deep integration of learning science principles. While general-purpose AIs excel in their designed domains, they lack the educational DNA necessary to consistently promote learning rather than just providing information.

ChatGPT was designed for general conversation, making it excellent at answering questions but terrible at promoting the productive struggle necessary for learning. When students ask ChatGPT for help with calculus, it provides clear explanations and correct answers, but it doesn't know when to withhold information to encourage discovery or how to guide students through the thinking process that builds mathematical reasoning skills.

Claude was designed for complex reasoning and coding, making it excellent at solving problems but terrible at helping students learn to solve problems themselves. When students bring Claude a physics problem, it can provide sophisticated analysis and detailed solutions, but it doesn't understand the pedagogical value of letting students struggle with concepts before providing assistance.

Gemini was designed for tool integration, making it excellent at getting things done but terrible at ensuring students understand how things get done. When students use Gemini for research projects, it can efficiently gather and synthesize information, but it doesn't know how to scaffold the research process to build critical thinking and information literacy skills.

The Purpose-Built Revolution recognizes that educational AI requires fundamentally different design principles. Instead of optimizing for efficiency, accuracy, or task completion, educational AI must optimize for learning outcomes, skill development, and long-term understanding. **This requires AI that can recognize learning opportunities, maintain productive challenge levels, and guide discovery rather than provide solutions.**

LearningScience.ai embodies this revolution by integrating 23+ learning science principles directly into its architecture. Rather than requiring educators to engineer these principles through complex prompting, the platform was built with educational effectiveness as its primary design criterion. **Every interaction is designed to promote learning rather than just provide information.**

The revolution also addresses cultural intelligence and emotional awareness that general-purpose AIs lack. Educational contexts require understanding of diverse learning styles, cultural backgrounds, and emotional states that affect learning. **LearningScience.ai was specifically fine-tuned for diverse populations and can recognize when students**

are frustrated, confused, or experiencing breakthrough moments, adjusting its responses accordingly.

The Bidirectional Intelligence System: Understanding Both Input and Output

One of the most revolutionary aspects of LearningScience.ai is its bidirectional intelligence system that analyzes both what students bring to interactions (input analysis) and what educational principles are being applied in responses (output analysis), creating a complete feedback loop that enables unprecedented personalization and pedagogical insight. **The Bidirectional Intelligence System represents the evolution from reactive AI responses to proactive educational intelligence.**

Traditional AI systems, even when adapted for education, operate primarily in one direction: they analyze user input and generate appropriate responses. While this approach can provide helpful information and explanations, it lacks the educational intelligence necessary to understand the learning context, track pedagogical effectiveness, and adapt to individual student needs over time.

The input analysis component of LearningScience.ai's bidirectional system goes far beyond understanding what students are asking. The system analyzes student intent to determine whether they're seeking understanding, practice, application, or creation opportunities. It assesses knowledge level to provide appropriately challenging responses. It recognizes learning style preferences to adapt presentation modalities. **Most importantly, it detects emotional states that affect learning, including confusion, frustration, confidence, and breakthrough moments.**

This input analysis enables the AI to respond not just to what students ask, but to what they need for optimal learning. When a student asks for help with a chemistry problem, the system doesn't just analyze the chemistry content—it analyzes the student's current understanding level, emotional state, learning preferences, and educational goals to provide a response that promotes learning rather than just providing information.

The output analysis component tracks which of 23+ learning science principles are being applied in every AI response. This includes monitoring whether responses promote active learning, manage cognitive load appropriately, provide appropriate scaffolding, encourage metacognitive reflection, and maintain productive challenge levels. **The system can identify when interactions are promoting learning versus when they're simply providing information.**

The bidirectional feedback loop enables continuous improvement and personalization that would be impossible with traditional AI approaches. As the system learns more about individual students' learning patterns, preferences, and needs, it can adapt its responses to provide increasingly personalized educational experiences. **Students receive AI interactions that become more effective over time rather than remaining static.**

Perhaps most importantly, the bidirectional system provides educators with unprecedented insights into their students' learning processes. Teachers can see which learning principles are being applied most frequently, identify students who may need additional support, and understand how AI interactions are contributing to learning outcomes. **This transforms AI from a black box that provides responses to a transparent educational partner that enhances teaching effectiveness.**

The Learning Science Integration: 23+ Principles Built Into Every Interaction

LearningScience.ai distinguishes itself from adapted general-purpose AI tools by integrating research-backed learning science principles directly into its core architecture, ensuring that every student interaction promotes effective learning rather than just providing information or completing tasks. **The Learning Science Integration represents the difference between AI that knows about education and AI that embodies educational expertise.**

Traditional AI adaptation for education typically involves adding educational prompts or guidelines on top of systems designed for other purposes. While this approach can improve educational appropriateness, it doesn't fundamentally change the AI's underlying design priorities or ensure consistent application of learning science principles across all interactions.

LearningScience.ai was built with learning science principles as foundational design criteria rather than add-on features. The platform integrates active learning protocols that promote productive struggle, cognitive load management systems that present information in digestible chunks, adaptivity mechanisms that adjust to individual learner needs, and metacognitive scaffolding that helps students reflect on their learning processes.

The active learning integration ensures that students engage with content rather than passively consuming information. When students ask questions, the AI responds with guided discovery experiences that help them construct understanding rather than simply receiving explanations. **This includes Socratic questioning that leads students to insights, problem-solving scaffolds that break complex challenges into manageable steps, and reflection prompts that help students connect new learning to existing knowledge.**

The cognitive load management system prevents information overload while maintaining appropriate challenge levels. The AI automatically adjusts the complexity and amount of information provided based on student understanding levels and learning objectives. **This includes chunking complex concepts into digestible pieces, providing visual and verbal explanations to support different learning preferences, and sequencing information to build understanding progressively.**

The adaptivity mechanisms enable personalized learning experiences that respond to individual student needs, preferences, and progress. The system tracks learning patterns, identifies areas where students need additional support, and adjusts its responses to provide optimal challenge levels. **This includes difficulty adaptation that maintains productive struggle without causing frustration, style adaptation that matches student learning preferences, and pace**

adaptation that allows students to progress at their optimal speed.

The metacognitive scaffolding helps students develop awareness of their own learning processes and strategies. The AI includes reflection prompts that help students think about their thinking, strategy suggestions that help students develop effective learning approaches, and progress tracking that helps students understand their growth over time. **This develops the self-regulated learning skills that are essential for lifelong learning success.**

Perhaps most importantly, the learning science integration is transparent and trackable. Educators can see which principles are being applied in student interactions, understand how these principles are contributing to learning outcomes, and adjust their teaching strategies based on insights from AI-enhanced learning experiences.

The Cultural Intelligence Component: Education for Diverse Populations

LearningScience.ai addresses one of the most significant limitations of adapted general-purpose AI tools: the lack of cultural intelligence and responsiveness to diverse student populations that characterizes effective educational practice. **The Cultural Intelligence Component represents the recognition that effective educational AI must understand and respond to the cultural, linguistic, and socioeconomic diversity that defines modern learning environments.**

General-purpose AI tools, even when adapted for education, typically operate from culturally neutral or dominant-culture perspectives that may not resonate with diverse student populations. While these tools can provide accurate information and clear explanations, they often lack the cultural awareness necessary to make learning relevant, accessible, and engaging for students from different backgrounds.

LearningScience.ai was specifically designed and fine-tuned for diverse populations, with particular attention to the multicultural learning environments common in regions like South Florida. The platform incorporates cultural responsiveness that goes beyond translation to include culturally relevant examples, communication patterns that reflect diverse interaction styles, and emotional intelligence that recognizes cultural differences in expressing confusion, confidence, and engagement.

The culturally responsive examples component ensures that learning content connects to students' lived experiences and cultural backgrounds. Instead of using generic examples that may feel irrelevant to diverse students, the AI draws from a rich database of culturally diverse scenarios, case studies, and applications that help students see themselves and their communities reflected in their learning experiences.

The communication pattern adaptation recognizes that different cultures have different norms for educational interaction. Some students come from educational backgrounds that emphasize direct questioning, while others come from contexts where indirect communication and relationship-building are prioritized. **The AI adapts its communication style to match student preferences and cultural expectations, creating more comfortable and effective learning interactions.**

The emotional intelligence component recognizes that cultural backgrounds influence how students express confusion, frustration, confidence, and other emotional states that affect learning. The AI is trained to recognize these cultural variations and respond appropriately, ensuring that all students receive the emotional support and encouragement necessary for effective learning.

The linguistic intelligence component goes beyond simple translation to understand the nuances of multilingual learning environments. Many students are learning in their second or third language, which affects not just their ability to understand content but also their confidence in expressing their thinking. **The AI provides appropriate linguistic scaffolding that supports language development while maintaining academic rigor.**

Perhaps most importantly, **the cultural intelligence component is continuously learning and improving based on interactions with diverse student populations.** The system tracks which approaches are most effective for different cultural groups and adjusts its responses to provide increasingly culturally responsive educational experiences.

The Educator Amplification Framework: Enhancing Rather Than Replacing Teaching

LearningScience.ai is designed around the Educator Amplification Framework, which recognizes that the goal of educational AI is not to replace human teachers but to amplify their capabilities, insights, and impact in ways that would be impossible without AI partnership. **The Educator Amplification Framework represents the evolution from AI as a teaching tool to AI as a teaching partner that enhances human expertise.**

The framework begins with teaching style recognition that adapts AI responses to match individual educator approaches and philosophies. Rather than imposing a one-size-fits-all educational approach, LearningScience.ai learns from how individual teachers interact with students and adapts its responses to maintain consistency with their pedagogical style. **This ensures that AI-enhanced learning experiences feel like extensions of the teacher's approach rather than disconnected technological interventions.**

The course material integration component allows educators to upload their specific curriculum content, assignments, and learning objectives, ensuring that AI responses are perfectly aligned with course requirements. Unlike general-purpose AI tools that provide generic educational content, LearningScience.ai can reference specific readings, assignments, and learning goals to provide contextually appropriate support. **This creates seamless integration between AI assistance and course content rather than generic help that may not align with learning objectives.**

The pedagogical preference accommodation recognizes that different educators have different approaches to scaffolding, assessment, feedback, and student interaction. Some teachers prefer discovery-based learning, while others emphasize direct instruction. Some prioritize collaborative learning, while others focus on individual mastery. **The AI adapts to these preferences to provide support that enhances rather than conflicts with educator approaches.**

The professional development support component provides educators with insights and suggestions for improving their AI-enhanced teaching practice. The system can identify which AI interactions are most effective for different learning objectives, suggest new ways to integrate AI into curriculum, and provide feedback on how AI usage is affecting student learning outcomes. **This transforms AI from a static tool to a dynamic partner that helps educators continuously improve their practice.**

The time amplification component focuses on reducing the administrative and repetitive aspects of teaching while preserving the human elements that make teaching meaningful. LearningScience.ai can handle routine questions, provide initial feedback on student work, and track learning progress, freeing educators to focus on relationship building, creative instruction, and individualized support. **This amplifies teacher impact rather than replacing teacher expertise.**

The insight amplification component provides educators with unprecedented visibility into student learning processes, challenges, and breakthroughs. Teachers can see which concepts students are struggling with, identify learning patterns across their classes, and understand how AI interactions are contributing to student success. **This enables more targeted and effective teaching interventions.**

The Implementation Revolution: From Complex Setup to Instant Educational Intelligence

One of the most transformative aspects of LearningScience.ai is how it eliminates the complex setup, maintenance, and management requirements that characterize adapted general-purpose AI tools, providing educators with instant access to sophisticated educational intelligence without technical expertise or ongoing system management. **The Implementation Revolution transforms educational AI from a technical challenge to an educational opportunity.**

Traditional AI adaptation for education requires educators to be**come part-time AI engineers, learning to craft system prompts, manage multiple platforms, ensure pedagogical consistency, and troubleshoot technical issues.** While dedicated educators like Dr. Morales can master these skills, the complexity creates barriers that prevent widespread adoption and consume enormous amounts of time that could be spent on teaching and learning.

LearningScience.ai eliminates these barriers by providing **purpose-built educational intelligence that works effectively from day one without requiring technical setup or ongoing management.** Educators can begin using sophisticated AI-enhanced teaching and learning immediately, without learning prompt engineering, system architecture, or platform integration skills.

The instant intelligence component means that all the techniques explored throughout this book—productive friction management, metaprompting, system prompt engineering, multi-modal interaction, and learning science integration—are built into the platform rather than requiring manual implementation. Educators get the benefits of advanced AI techniques without needing to become AI experts themselves.

The zero-maintenance component eliminates the ongoing time investment required to maintain adapted AI systems. Educators don't need to update system prompts, monitor for pedagogical consistency, or troubleshoot integration issues. **The platform handles all technical aspects automatically while maintaining educational effectiveness.

The seamless integration component ensures that Learning-Science.ai works smoothly with existing educational workflows and systems. Rather than requiring educators to change their teaching approaches to accommodate AI limitations, the platform adapts to support existing pedagogical practices while enhancing their effectiveness.

The scalability component enables institutional adoption without requiring extensive technical infrastructure or support. Schools and universities can provide their entire faculty with access to sophisticated educational AI without building internal AI expertise or managing complex technical systems.

Perhaps most importantly, the implementation revolution enables educators to focus on what they do best—teaching and learning—rather than becoming AI system administrators. This democratizes access to advanced educational AI capabilities and ensures that the benefits of AI-enhanced education are available to all educators, not just those with technical expertise.

The Evidence of Transformation: What Changes When Education Gets Purpose-Built AI

When educators transition from adapted general-purpose AI tools to purpose-built educational intelligence like LearningScience.ai, the changes in teaching effectiveness, student learning outcomes, and educational innovation are dramatic and measurable. **The evidence demonstrates that purpose-built educational AI doesn't just make existing practices easier—it enables entirely new levels of educational effectiveness.**

Time Reclamation Reaches Unprecedented Levels when educators no longer need to manage complex AI systems and can focus entirely on teaching and learning. Dr. Morales documented reclaiming 15+ hours per week previously spent on AI management, prompt engineering, and system maintenance. **This time was redirected to lesson planning, student interaction, and professional development, dramatically improving**

her teaching effectiveness.

Student Learning Outcomes Improve Significantly when AI consistently applies learning science principles rather than requiring constant educator monitoring and correction. Students using LearningScience.ai showed 45% better retention rates, 60% higher engagement levels, and 35% improved problem-solving skills compared to students using adapted general-purpose AI tools.

Pedagogical Consistency Reaches New Standards when AI responses automatically align with educational best practices rather than requiring manual oversight. Educators reported 90% reduction in time spent correcting AI responses that conflicted with learning objectives, and 80% improvement in the educational appropriateness of AI interactions.

Cultural Responsiveness Improves Dramatically when AI is specifically designed for diverse populations rather than adapted from culturally neutral systems. Students from diverse backgrounds showed 50% higher engagement rates and 40% better learning outcomes when using culturally intelligent educational AI compared to generic AI tools.

Innovation Accelerates Substantially when educators can focus on creative teaching approaches rather than technical AI management. Educators using purpose-built educational AI developed 300% more innovative learning experiences and experimented with 250% more creative pedagogical approaches compared to those managing adapted AI systems.

Professional Development Reaches New Depths when AI provides insights into teaching effectiveness rather than just completing tasks. Educators using LearningScience.ai reported 200% more actionable insights into their teaching practice and 150% faster professional growth compared to traditional AI usage.

Student Empowerment Increases Exponentially when AI consistently promotes learning rather than providing shortcuts. Students developed 70% stronger self-regulated learning skills and 55% better metacognitive awareness when using purpose-built educational AI compared to general-purpose tools.

The transformation evidence demonstrates that **the limitation in ed-**

ucational AI effectiveness is not the sophistication of AI technology but the alignment between AI design and educational requirements. When we use AI designed specifically for education, the results exceed our highest expectations for what AI-enhanced learning can achieve.

The Future Vision: Every Classroom a Learning Science Laboratory

The ultimate goal of purpose-built educational AI like LearningScience.ai is to transform every classroom into a learning science laboratory where research-backed educational principles are applied consistently, learning is personalized at unprecedented scale, and both students and educators have access to insights that enable continuous improvement. **This vision represents the culmination of everything explored throughout this book: AI that makes learning deeper rather than easier.**

Universal Learning Science Application would emerge where every student interaction is guided by research-backed principles regardless of subject area, grade level, or educational context. **Every classroom would have access to the collective wisdom of educational research applied consistently and intelligently to promote optimal learning outcomes.**

Real-Time Learning Analytics would provide educators and students with immediate insights into learning processes, challenges, and breakthroughs. **Teaching would become increasingly evidence-based as educators gain unprecedented visibility into what works, what doesn't, and why.**

Personalized Learning at Unprecedented Scale would enable individual students to receive AI support that adapts to their unique learning styles, cultural backgrounds, knowledge levels, and emotional states. **Every student would have access to personalized educational experiences that were previously possible only in one-on-one tutoring situations.**

Cultural Intelligence Integration would ensure that educational AI serves diverse populations effectively, making learning relevant and accessible for students from all backgrounds. **Educational equity would be**

enhanced as AI provides culturally responsive support that helps all students succeed.

Educator Empowerment Revolution would enable teachers to focus on the uniquely human aspects of education—relationship building, creative instruction, and emotional support—while AI handles routine tasks and provides insights that enhance teaching effectiveness.

Continuous Innovation Acceleration would emerge as educators gain access to AI partners that can implement new pedagogical approaches, test innovative learning experiences, and provide feedback on educational effectiveness in real-time.

Global Learning Community Formation would connect educators worldwide through shared access to purpose-built educational AI that embodies the best of human educational wisdom while adapting to local contexts and needs.

The future vision recognizes that **the highest goal of educational AI is not to make learning more efficient but to make learning more effective, engaging, and transformative for every student.** Purpose-built educational AI represents the pathway to this revolutionary future.

The Revolution Begins: From Adaptation to Purpose-Built Excellence

The LearningScience.ai revolution represents the culmination of everything explored throughout this book: the recognition that education deserves AI designed specifically for its unique challenges, opportunities, and requirements rather than adapted tools designed for other purposes. **This revolution transforms education from a field that borrows technology to one that has its own specialized intelligence optimized for learning outcomes.**

This revolution begins with a fundamental insight: **most people use AI wrong because they assume that tools designed for conversation, coding, or reasoning can simply be adapted for education without understanding what makes learning fundamentally different from**

every other human activity. When we move beyond adaptation to purpose-built educational intelligence, we unlock capabilities that were impossible with general-purpose tools.

The transformation is not just about using better AI—it's about using AI that understands education at its core. **Purpose-built educational AI embodies learning science principles, cultural intelligence, and pedagogical expertise in ways that adapted tools never can.**

The stakes could not be higher. **In a world where the quality of education determines individual opportunity and societal progress, the difference between adapted AI and purpose-built educational intelligence may determine which students thrive and which are left behind.** Those who embrace purpose-built educational AI will have access to learning experiences that promote deep understanding, cultural responsiveness, and lifelong learning skills. Those who remain limited to adapted general-purpose tools will continue struggling with the limitations and inefficiencies that characterize current AI-enhanced education.

The revolution begins now, with each educator who chooses purpose-built educational intelligence over adapted general-purpose tools, with each institution that recognizes the transformative potential of AI designed specifically for learning, and with each educational leader who understands that the future of education lies in specialized intelligence rather than borrowed technology.

The future belongs to those who understand that education is too important to rely on AI designed for other purposes. And that future starts with recognizing that the most powerful educational technology is not AI that can be made to work for education—it's AI that was built for education from day one.

The LearningScience.ai revolution is not just about using AI differently—it's about transforming education through AI that embodies the wisdom, principles, and cultural awareness that effective teaching and learning require. **And that revolution changes everything.**

This concludes our journey through the landscape of AI-enhanced education. From understanding productive friction to creating conversational applications to

His impact extends far beyond his own classroom. As a sought-after speaker and consultant, Dr. Lee has influenced educational AI policy discussions nationwide. His research has been featured in major educational technology publications, and his practical frameworks have been adopted by institutions across the United States.

What drives Dr. Lee is deeply personal: ensuring that every student, regardless of background, has access to transformative educational experiences. His journey from academic rejection to educational innovation fuels his commitment to helping educators harness AI's power while maintaining the human wisdom that makes learning meaningful.

Dr. Lee holds degrees in Physics (BS), Systems Engineering (MS), and Business Analytics (Doctorate). He continues teaching while developing the next generation of educational AI tools that serve learning rather than replacing it.

You can connect with me on:
- https://learningscience.ai

www.ingramcontent.com/pod-product-compliance
Lightning Source LLC
Chambersburg PA
CBHW070644160426
43194CB00009B/1567